ANCHORED IN LIGHT

To Lynnie,

To win the day,
endure the night!!

Carl P

ANCHORED IN LIGHT

UNDERSTANDING AND OVERCOMING
THE FIVE DEADLIEST THREATS
TO YOUR FAITH

CARL EDWIN PRUDE JR.

LEAFWOOD
PUBLISHERS

ANCHORED IN LIGHT
Understanding and Overcoming the Five Deadliest Threats to Your Faith

Copyright 2013 by Carl Prude.

ISBN 978-0-89112-347-7
LCCN 2013023001

Printed in the United States of America

All scripture quotations, unless otherwise indicated, are taken from the New King James Version®. Copyright © 1982 by Thomas Nelson, Inc. Used by permission. All rights reserved. Scripture quotations marked AMP are taken from the Amplified Bible. Copyright © 1954, 1958, 1962, 1964, 1965, 1987 by the Lockman Foundation. Used by permission. Scripture quotations marked ESV are from The Holy Bible, English Standard Version, copyright © 2001 by Crossway, a publishing ministry of Good News Publishers. Used by permission. All rights reserved. Scripture quotations marked HCSB are been taken from the Holman Christian Standard Bible, Copyright © 1999, 2000, 2002, 2003 by Holman Bible Publishers. Used by permission. Scripture quotations marked MSG are from The Message. Copyright © 1993, 1994, 1995, 1996, 2000, 2001, 2002. Used by permission of NavPress Publishing Group.

Printed in association with The Seymour Agency, 475 Miner Street Road, Canton, New York 13617

LIBRARY OF CONGRESS CATALOGING-IN-PUBLICATION DATA
Prude, Carl, Jr., 1958-
  Anchored in light : understanding and overcoming the five deadliest threats to your faith / Carl Prude, Jr.
    pages cm
  Includes bibliographical references and index.
  ISBN 978-0-89112-347-7 (alk. paper)
  1. Christian life. 2. Christianity and culture. 3. Christianity--21st century. I. Title.
  BV4501.3.P78 2013
  248.4--dc23
                                                                              2013023001

Cover design by Thinkpen Design, LLC
Interior text design by Sandy Armstrong

Leafwood Publishers 1626 Campus Court
Abilene, Texas 79601 1-877-816-4455 toll free

For current information about all Leafwood titles, visit our Web site:
www.leafwoodpublishers.com

13 14 15 16 17 18 / 7 6 5 4 3 2 1

Table of Contents

To my parents,

Carl E. Prude Sr. and Lillie B. Prude.
My biggest heroes, first mentors, enduring role models,
and two closest friends.

ACKNOWLEDGMENTS

This book is the product of the efforts of many talented and wonderful people whose contributions stood up and stood out during the course of this writing journey.

First, I want to thank two amazing mentors; award winning authors Kathi Macias and Sharon Ewell-Foster. Thank you for helping me understand the mechanics of the publishing industry, and for modeling what it means to be a professional writer.

Thanks to the best literary agent on the planet, Mary Sue Seymour (I have indisputable evidence to back this claim) and the incredibly talented staff of the Seymour Agency.

Thanks to Dr. Leonard Allen and the incredibly talented Leafwood Publishers family.

I'd like to thank my mom, Mrs. Lillie B. Prude, and my seven siblings (Avis, Mark, Vian, Lili, Dona, Paul and Dwan) for their support, love, and weekly conference calls.

I want to thank my "sounding boards" for their timely insight and inspired counsel, in particular Bishop Robert Hooks, Bishop Raphael Green, Ron Harden, and J. Norbert McDaniels.

I thank the teachers and leaders who helped keep me fed, focused, and healthy throughout this process, particularly Jack Hayford, Jim and Debbie Cobrae, Bishop Joseph and Barbara Garlington, and Bishop Noel Jones.

I give special acknowledgment to Mother Trudy Lewis (my grandmother), and Bishop Benjamin and Mrs. Catherine Crouch for their love, time, prayers, and personal investment in my life.

Music has always been part of the creative process for me, and I want to acknowledge the musical artists I leaned on during the three years it took to bring this product to market: Andrae and Sandra Crouch, Kelly Willard, Van Burchfield, Danniebelle Hall, Koinonia, Donald Lawrence, Jay Leach, Mitchell Jones, Jonathon Butler, Sarah Jordan Powell, Earl Klugh, Brenda Roy, Kristle Murden, and Stefanie Kelly. Your music quieted my soul and awakened my ear to hear as the learned.

I thank my older brother-from-another-mother, Stewart Roberts for staying up many nights well past 1 A.M. to listen to whatever I was rambling about (and his dear wife Susan for letting him stay up).

I want to thank my three amazing children (Carl III, Carlina, and Carlton) for their patience, support, and understanding during the writing of this book.

Finally, I want to thank God who gave me life, health, dreams, and a heart that beats for His best in other people.

INTRODUCTION

The book you're holding will help you make sense of the world you live in, and in particular many of the things happening in the faith community today. It will help you regain your spiritual footing and rediscover the indispensable and unconquerable joy that's the by-product of genuine spiritual health.

This book will help you connect the dots between faith and future, past and present, hope and anguish, and reality and life. It will give you the tools you need to finish well. But, before we get to that, allow me to share the story behind the story—how this book came into being.

It all started on the winter solstice of 2008, when I awoke at 4:15 a.m. with five phrases floating around in my head: *Space Yourself, Pace Yourself, Waste Yourself, Place Yourself,* and *Grace Yourself.* I'm a songwriter, among other things, and many of my songs start out as dreams, so I just assumed these phrases were going to end up as lyrics for an upcoming song. Boy was I wrong.

Four weeks after this incident, I got a call from my sister with the news that my dad had passed away. He fought an extended five-year battle with several serious diseases. He underwent amputations, heart procedures, and endured a variety of medical treatments at all kinds of facilities. Sometimes I felt he was being used as a human pincushion, but in the end his body couldn't keep up with a spirit that refused to quit.

I knew the phone call would eventually come, but when it finally came, it left me unexpectedly numb—just numb.

My dad and I were very close. He was my role model, mentor, hero, and friend. He was a war veteran and a bi-vocational pastor. He worked as a manager with the U.S. Postal Service (retiring after twenty-seven years), and served in pastoral ministry for almost fifty years. He was successful in all his vocations, with accomplishments too numerous to list. He was a phenomenal pastor, an even better father, and perhaps an even better husband.

I was still adjusting to his death when, a couple of days later, my family asked me to give the eulogy at his funeral. I've presided over dozens of funerals, but when it came to preparing for this one, I was at a complete loss. Not only was I unable to come up with a basic outline for the eulogy, I couldn't even put a single sentence together.

I tried to put together something fitting for the occasion, but up to the night before the funeral, I still had nothing. I opened my notebook in another effort to prepare my remarks for the funeral. After staring at the same blank sheet of paper for almost an hour, I pushed my chair away from the table, tilted my head back as far as it would go, closed my eyes, and said a very simple prayer: "God, I need your help."

That's when the five phrases from the dream resurfaced in my mind. Having nothing better to think about at the time, I began rolling those phrases around in my head—not connecting them with my dad in any way. After a few minutes I was about to dismiss them when it struck me that these phrases weren't the lyrics to an unwritten song, but, in fact, represented five significant pillars of my dad's life.

- Space yourself represented his resilient ability to trust God through good or bad.
- Pace yourself represented his skill in remaining aligned with his calling and purpose—even as the seasons of his life changed drastically.
- Waste yourself represented the way he processed life's hardships or mistreatment from others. He never allowed the pain of unforgiveness, emotional scarring, or mental anguish to establish a foothold in his life.
- Place yourself symbolized his enduring celebration of who and how God had made him. He appreciated who he was and was wonderfully content in his own skin.
- Finally, Grace yourself represented the spiritual foundations that created continuous momentum throughout his lifetime.

This was the eulogy I sought. While none of these principles were new, I hadn't seen anyone live them quite the way my dad had lived them. I hadn't seen them demonstrated collectively the way they were in his everyday life. With each passing year, he continued to grow and abound in them. Even as life came at him from all angles (as it does for all of us), he exercised these spiritual tenets and, as a result, his spiritual muscles grew stronger and stronger, even as his body grew weaker and weaker.

The day of my dad's funeral also happened to be the day of the worst snowstorm the Midwest had seen in over seventy-five years. In spite of this, the church couldn't hold all the people who tried to press into the building. The service was amazing, lasting six hours, and the eulogy provided the kind of send-off I know would have pleased my dad.

About a month later, I was hiking alone through Southern California's Box Spring Mountains. I came to a beautiful pomegranate grove completely hidden from the world. I stopped to rest—and to pray. I felt heaviness in my heart as I thought on several unrelated, alarming situations concerning different individuals and congregations.

The community of faith was in the throes of a quiet storm, bombarded with conflicting teachings from every direction, bearing the stretch marks from accommodating things like church leaders who conduct themselves like pop stars, to the pressures of appearing irrelevant before a generation with diminishing appreciation for time-honored spiritual standards.

In the face of the unique challenges of twenty-first century living, the faith community was starting to fray and unravel like a well-worn sweater. Believers were drifting and faith was waning (although you'd be hard-pressed to get people to admit it openly). It seemed as if everywhere I went, every month there was a new focus, every week a new word, every day a new confession.

These signs masked a more serious problem that existed at the core of believers' lives. I sat down on a mountain rock, and my heart became heavy. I felt the burden and the pain of many people who were lost—not in the world, but in the church. Lost in faith.

As I reflected on my own experiences as a pastor, counseling and praying with so many people, I noticed five distinct patterns of spiritual malfunction that seemed common to most of these situations—in individual lives as well as among groups. As I contemplated these things, I realized they weren't simply malfunctions; they were planned attacks. They were five threats—deadly threats—intentionally designed to destabilize people of faith. And they were working.

As I sat there alone, I prayed. I wept. I interceded. My heart ached.

Slowly, I began to understand that people in the faith community were falling prey to these attacks because many of their lives weren't anchored properly. Their hopes were in contemporary religious values that had emerged from the midst of a declining, irreligious culture. I prayed, asking God to correct the situation.

That's when I saw it. That's when everything that had happened during the past two months suddenly started making sense. The five principles of my dad's life provided the answers I looked for. They were the anchors that so many people desperately needed.

In the days to come, I began to share these tenets during speaking, counseling, and prayer sessions. I shared them with pastors and leaders within the faith community. The results were simply amazing. Situations (as well as individual lives) slowly transformed right before my eyes—a direct result of applying these spiritual anchors.

It was then I knew this message could bring relief to many who were struggling in their walk of faith. I felt the best way to reach them was to put everything in a book; you're holding that book today.

My prayer is that the book reaches those who need to hear its message—those drifting in faith, whose spiritual foundations have become unstable.

My dad was a true pastor—a man with a shepherd's heart. In many ways, this is his final message to the people he loved and the God he served. In living, he gave me his name. In dying, he gave me his legacy.

I now share this message and legacy with you, and encourage you to anchor yourselves to the truths that emanate from the foundations of creation, and to the light that illuminates both time and timelessness.

Carl Edwin Prude Jr.

Nevertheless the solid foundation
of God stands, having this seal:

"The Lord knows those who are His" (2 Tim. 2:19)

Chapter 1

LOST IN FAITH

Paradox in Paradise

Faith.

Faith is God's watermark on the universe. It's his thumbprint. It quietly maps his movements with unmistaken accuracy. Where he's been, where he is, and where he's going.

By faith we press our faces against the clouded window of the supernatural realm—fogged over on one side from our anxious intercessions, misted on the other by God's reassuring breath from what he's spoken.

By faith our eternal destination is re-assigned. With it we overcome life's obstacles and possess life's promises. The broken parts of our lives are made whole by faith. Faith is a prized seed that has to be cultivated diligently, because all seekers ultimately must learn to live by faith intimately.

But I have a question for those of us who belong to the community of faith: Is our faith failing us today?

Consider recent statistics show that certain social behaviors (once reliable indicators of the distinctions between believers and nonbelievers) now point to lifestyles running at a virtual dead heat. For instance, in the United States the divorce rate for first marriages among non-churchgoers is about 44%. How does that compare to the divorce rate for first marriages among church attendees? About 42%—too close for comfort. Other studies show that some of the highest divorce rates in the country aren't found in liberal states like California or New York, but in Tennessee, Arkansas, Missouri and Oklahoma—the heart of America's conservative "Bible Belt."[1] Most of us would have thought the opposite to be the case.

Similarly, regarding other bellwether social practices ranging from premarital sex to drinking to lying, polls show the gap closing fast between the conduct of believers and non-believers.[2]

Of course moral fidelity isn't the only yardstick for spiritual fitness; still, these trends are saying something we can't afford to ignore. In fact, they should disturb us enough to cause us to drop our hymnals, cough up our communion wafer, and wonder out loud, *"What in hell is going on in our churches?"*

Take a moment and answer the following question honestly: Which bothers you most; the razor-thin margin between the life-styles of believers and non-believers, or the phrase, "What in hell is going on in our churches?"

Remember, these statistics aren't just faceless numbers on a piece of paper—they represent *millions* of *real people* whose spiritual experiences just *aren't* fully working for them. On the other hand, the undeniable sway of modern culture in the faith community is much more an indication of where we're headed based on where they're headed, than where we should be going based on where we've come from. Whatever your answer is, there's clearly something wrong. But what?

Perhaps Rick Warren's runaway best seller, *The Purpose Driven Life*, gives us a clue. It exposed a surprising hunger for identity and purpose among people of faith—surprising because for thousands of years neither our purpose nor our identity has changed. As people of faith our purpose has always been simple: to honor God by allowing his light to shine in and through us to every internal and external place where darkness still has influence. Our identity is equally clear; we all share an unmistakable birthmark—a logo so unnatural that the Romans who first observed it had to develop a word just to describe it—*agapao*.[3]

We need to look deeper to understand exactly what people in today's faith community are really hungering for. What do we see as our actual purpose, identity, and priorities?

It's not such a simple answer, mainly because today's faith community is as complicated as it is wonderful. For example, some see their priority as their family. For others, it's their set of religious beliefs. For still others, it's their particular church community.

One assembly regards healing and miracles as the benchmark for spiritual validation, another looks at community service and missions, while still another sees it as rising social status or material gain.

One group's meetings center on the worship and praise experience, another's emphasizes evangelism, while still another group focuses on spectacular, supernatural demonstrations.

From our pulpits we're presented with as much variety as a Skittles factory; sermon styles ranging from mono-droning lectures that force us to dig our fingernails deep into our thigh just to stay alert, to caffeinated screaming about something so abstract the speaker doesn't even bother to connect it to a scriptural text.

All these expressions flow from the handiwork of a God who loves minutes and millenniums, the ordinary and the extraordinary, and silence as much as noise.

To the casual observer, today's faith community is all over the place—but in a sense that's okay, because at times life *really is* all over the place. Still, so much divergence within the faith community has added to a gradual erosion of the believers' once clear spiritual identity. Our efforts to keep pace with each new spiritual trend has left many of our spiritual identities so smudged that they're nearly unrecognizable—like a homework assignment that's been crumpled, tossed out the window, run over by a muddy tire, and left in a wet drain ditch.

Some try to dismiss these developments with clichés like, "the church is just getting worldlier and the world is getting churchier." On the surface there appears to be some truth to this, but a closer look shows this to be just an excuse that sidesteps the real issue. After all, people in "the world" aren't expected to have it together in the first place—the same can't be said for people who've been called "the light of the world."

As children of eternal hope, we all want to finish our races strongly, anticipating the words that will make our efforts all worth it: "Well done, my good and faithful servant." But too many believers today are closer to throwing up their hands in frustration and saying, "that's it, *I'm done!*", than they are to hearing, "*well done.*" It's a problem that's simply gotten too big and too ugly to ignore.

In an effort to regain their lost spiritual equilibrium, people of faith change churches, change worship habits, change devotional routines, and even change faiths. These tactics don't work because they don't get to the root of the problem.

This book pierces through all the religious formality and temple smoke, and uncovers the roots of the current spiritual crisis. More importantly, it provides a clear pathway forward for people of faith everywhere.

What's Really Troubling the Waters?

Exactly what has doused the flame on the altar for so many people in today's faith community? The simple answer is things that they've experienced—the hardships and complexities that don't fit neatly into a doctrinal box or philosophical slot. Here are some examples:

- "My doctor just diagnosed me with cancer, but before I could tell my wife, she announced that she's leaving me for someone else. How do I handle this?"
- "It seems like I've achieved everything I set out to do in life—so how come I feel more like killing myself instead of celebrating?"
- "I went through some terrible things as a child—now that I'm an adult how can I keep these memories from robbing me of the joys of life?"
- "Our church meetings feel more like a Multi-Level-Marketing rally than a worship service. The focus used to be the cross and the lost—lately I feel like *I'm lost*. I'm not sure where we're going or what we're doing!"
- "Everybody I'm around really tries to push me to do my best, *except* my family. They're *so* unsupportive and negative—and we're all supposed to be Christians! They throw a wet blanket on anything I try to do!"
- "I don't seem to enjoy our church services or women's group activities as much as the other women around me—I feel like I just don't fit in. Is there something wrong with me?"
- "Why are there so many ups and downs to life? When will things settle down for me?"
- "I've made some poor choices in life. I've owned up to them and, in some cases, paid a dear price. I really want to move on, but there are people close to me who just won't let me get beyond my past mistakes. I really care for them, but I wonder if it's time for me to just cut the ties with them and get a fresh start somewhere else?"

- "Our pastor divorced his wife and married another woman in the congregation. He taught so strongly about making marriage work—and now this! I feel bad about staying at this church, and even worse about leaving. How can I trust his leadership?"

- "My three-year old child died of heart disease. He suffered all of his short life, and although we prayed and fasted, it seemed like God just looked the other way. What was the point of all the pain this has caused for our family?"

- "It seems that only certain people at our church get 'blessed' all the time. New houses, new cars, raises on their jobs—the list just doesn't stop! I can't even pay my utility bills, and my car is about to be repossessed. I tithe and I'm a faithful volunteer in the children's ministry. Does God show favorites or is there just something wrong with my faith?"

- "One of our youth pastors was recently arrested and convicted of molesting young boys. I was horrified to discover my grandson was one of his victims! To rub salt in the wound, our church tried to cover it up for over a year. It was a major chore getting his parents to let him go to church with me in the first place. Now, not only has this destroyed my relationship with my daughter and son-in-law, but how can I forgive myself for what's happened to my own grandson?"

- "My older brother's been diagnosed with mental illness, but our church leaders insist that he's possessed by an evil spirit! They say he's brought it all on himself because he's never belonged to a church. They seem to have no idea what our family is really going through. I'm starting to hate these people!"

- "I've served as a leader in the church for over two decades. I have strained relationships with my family, my children don't want anything to do with church, and all the people I've tried to help over the years have run after the newest Christian fad. In all my years no one has ever come up to me and asked, 'Pastor, are you okay?' I know my reward is in heaven, but why do I feel so empty now?"

These questions all come from real situations involving real people, and they aren't uncommon in today's society. However, within the sanitized church community, where our expectations are different, they strike us with surprising force—like a vicious Mike Tyson blow to the sternum. They leave us desperately gasping for air, even in a faith environment where others are breathing just fine. It's these types of experiences that can cause us to lose our grip on our faith— especially if our pastors, priests, ministers, or spiritual leaders aren't well enough equipped to help us work through them.

These kinds of incidents jostle the hopes and derail the lives of countless believers, leaving them feeling that their faith amounts to little more than a handful of dried-out, crumbling Play-Doh.

Lost in Faith

What I've described in the previous paragraphs is a condition I call the *Lost in Faith Experience.* Here's a list of the most common symptoms:

- a sense of spiritual disillusionment
- a growing sense of spiritual frustration
- despondency about spiritual truths and realities
- new-founded doubts about scriptural authenticity
- apathy towards church-related activities that once provided joy and satisfaction

- a tendency to replace faith-centered activities with other activities
- an agitated attitude regarding spiritual topics
- a reluctance to participate in anything new in the faith community
- fragmented spiritual focus
- a diminished prayer life
- a general attitude of disappointment towards God
- detachment from friends within the faith community
- boredom with matters of spirituality

But here's one of the most compelling traits of the Lost in Faith Experience—these believers, though adrift, still love God, and don't want to abandon their faith altogether. Although *discontent* in their faith, they're not *disconnecting* from their faith. They're trying to hold on and gut it out, even though their spiritual lives aren't satisfying.

If you can identify with any of what I've described, don't feel discouraged—you're not alone. This Lost in Faith Experience is more prevalent among people of faith than those within the faith community understand—or are willing to admit.

For example, recent polls show that as many as 70% of all members of Christian-related churches say they're not satisfied with their spiritual lives. 70% of *anything* is high, and in this case it's alarming. This number represents a surge that sweeps past the borders of denomination, race, gender and age. Scores of believers, caught in its wake, are stranded with unsure footing and an unclear pathway forward.

Finally, here's help.

The Five Furies

For nearly two decades it's been my privilege to serve in different leadership roles within this wondrous faith community. I've served as a church planter, founded two non-profit religious community organizations, held the positions of senior pastor, associate pastor, assistant pastor, as well as several regional and local positions as director of this or that.

But for me, it's never been about the office or the title; it's always been about the *people*. I've shared many moments of public joy with people from all walks of life, and just as many moments of private sorrow. I've seen the sacred as well as the strange. I've sat in church business meetings with other pastors who had loaded pistols in their briefcases (in case the meeting didn't go the way they wanted), and I've sat at somber bedsides with families as a loved one closed her eyes for the last time and slipped into eternity.

No matter the situation or who was involved, I've always been driven by one thing: the possibility of helping one more person improve the quality of their life by improving the quality of their faith.

I can't count the counseling and prayer sessions I've had over the years with people who've lost their spiritual traction and fallen prey to this Lost in Faith Experience. Sometimes these meetings were formal appointments, but in many cases they were impromptu encounters that happened in a parking lot, in the bleachers at a high school football game, or on an early morning jog.

In my prayerful, continual search for answers, I began to notice five distinct, harmful patterns emerge—five murky but unmistakable recurring syndromes. In every instance where people had fallen victim to the Lost in Faith Experience, at least one of these patterns was a factor. In many cases, two or more were present.

In time, it became clear that the frequent appearance of these patterns wasn't just coincidental, nor was it merely symptomatic. These patterns were at the very root of the Lost in Faith Experience. The Lost in Faith Experience flowed out of them—not the other way around. I call these five troubling syndromes the *Five Furies*.

The "Fury" label comes from a reference found in the last book of the Bible: "But woe to the earth and the sea, because the devil has gone down to you! He is filled *with fury* [italics added], because he knows that his time is short" (Rev. 12:12).

The word "fury" in this passage is translated from the original Greek word, *thumos. Thumos* was commonly used in classical Greek language to describe the violent movement of nature, air (i.e., a violent tornado), water (i.e. a devastating tsunami), or land (i.e. a powerful earthquake). It's an unavoidable, destructive force that damages anything in its path.

In his epic work, *The Iliad*, Homer uses the word *thumos* to describe the uncontrollable wrath of Achilles, the poem's ruthless main character. When applied to living beings, *thumos* portrays a deep, driving rage that consumes its host, often taking them over the edge of insanity. *Thumos* is the worst kind of uncontrollable boiling rage. It's the kind of bad happening we can feel and see coming from miles away.

The Five Furies represent Satan's rage, and they carry all the destructive force that the word *thumos* implies. They ruin lives and destroy the things around us that we hold dear. However, unlike a hurricane or a tidal wave, we hardly ever see them coming. They don't register on a spiritual Richter scale like a violent earthquake. No, they're unassuming and deceptively quiet—their danger smolders beneath a non-threatening appearance.

Part of their genius is in their design. Remember, they come from the heart of Satan, and it's important to understand that above everything else, Satan is a lying deceiver. From his introduction in the Garden of Eden, Satan's nature has been deceptive: "the serpent deceived Eve by his craftiness" (see 2 Cor. 11:3). The very last time he's mentioned in the Bible he's still described as a deceiver; "The devil, who deceived them" (Rev. 20:10). His deceptive personality is changeless and unredeemable. These Furies represent his nature well.

He sends these destructive furies into the faith community in unmarked packages. They don't look like something we'd typically guard against (i.e., adultery, domestic violence, uncleanness, lasciviousness, idol worship, witchcraft, etc.). In fact, they don't necessarily look like . . . anything.

They have all the appearance of normal everyday life; nothing out of the ordinary, nothing to cause a raised eyebrow. Once they arrive we allow them to stay because we didn't see them coming.

When left undetected, each fury goes to work with deadly patience. Systematically, they produce microscopic punctures in our spiritual makeup. Unholy pinholes. These punctures become spiritual *leak-points* through which the virtue God gives us to overcome life's challenges slowly leaks out. Like a flattened tire with no visible signs of damage, we lose our ability to retain our inspiration.

When one of these furies is working in our lives, no matter how much time we spend praying, studying, or pouring out our hearts in worship services—the benefits of these activities don't last long enough to positively impact our lives. When we find ourselves in need, we turn to draw from these wells of virtue, only to find that our buckets are leaking.

The Five Furies convert stable believers into leaky people—people who look godly, but respond to situations in a worldly manner. These Furies are as unassuming as they are lethal. I consider them five of the deadliest threats facing the twenty-first century faith community. Let's take a look at each one briefly.

Fury #1: *Processing without Progressing*
Each day comes with a buffet of circumstances, choices, and challenges. Blessings as well as misfortunes. Things we anticipate as well as things out of the clear blue. Good as well as bad. Each of these occurrences needs to be addressed properly, and when we don't handle them properly they tend to collect into cluttered piles stuffed

into the corners of our souls. These piles undermine our sense of peace, wear away at our ability to fully enjoy our accomplishments and blessings, and make it difficult for us to find stability in our walk of faith. The Processing without Progressing Fury leaves the believer feeling lost, inept, and despondent.

Fury #2: *Running When You Should Be Walking and Walking When You Should Be Running*
This occurs when people of faith don't have a sense of peace about the use of their time, resources, and talents. They constantly anguish over projects and activities, always glancing over their shoulders for the better choice. They persistently second guess themselves while agonizing over whether their activities harmonize with God's will for them.

Am I running ahead of God or lagging behind him? Am I in step or out of step with his timing for me? Have I missed my "season"? The Running When You Should Be Walking and Walking When You Should Be Running Fury leaves believers feeling anxious, out-of-step with God's perfect will for them, and prodigal. They worry about running out of time before they've done what they were put on the earth to do.

Fury #3: *Entrenched in Stench*
This Fury involves mental or emotional baggage firmly lodged in a person's life, leaving one spiritually crippled. This baggage comes in two main flavors: unhealed wounds from the past, and new toxic experiences. Old junk and new garbage, either of which can be devastating to the life of faith.

While believers try to hide behind painted-on smiles and upbeat religious clichés, the betraying stench of this garbage still leaks through. The Entrenched in Stench Fury leaves the believer with a broad range of unhealthy perspectives—from bitterness, to anger, to low self-esteem, to hatred, to blaming others for their own chronic dissatisfactions—the list is virtually endless. People suffering from this Fury often have a sense of unresolved pain that offsets any other achievement in life, no matter how impressive. They often feel pessimistic and mentally paralyzed.

Fury #4: *The Assimilation Mutation*

This Fury represents the typical but harmful one-size-fits-all approach to service within the faith community. As members look to become more involved, they're often squeezed into old molds. Their spiritual identity and individuality is often shoved out of sight in the process. True, they're busy. Yes, they're productive. But they're also stifled, which leads to disheartenment—and they can't figure out why.

The Assimilation Mutation isn't typically part of a malicious plot, which makes it even more difficult to identify and resolve. For many believers, the eagerness to make themselves available for service within the faith community is the first step into a world in which they end up feeling used, manipulated, downgraded, and disregarded. The Assimilation Mutation leaves believers looking vogue on the outside, but feeling vague on the inside.

Fury #5: *Are We There Yet?*

This Fury represents the challenges associated with the gap between actual spiritual growth and our expectations for spiritual growth. People of faith spend thousands of hours in prayer, studying the scriptures, participating in worship services, and listening to sermons—only to discover that instead of actually "running" their races like well-trained athletes, their running style would more accurately be described as a stumble-thon towards the finish line—with plenty of scraped-up knees, banged elbows, and a few displaced teeth along the way.

Beset with recurring characters flaws, bound to certain bad habits, surprised at how easily they still react negatively when certain buttons are pushed, unable to consistently walk in certain disciplines of faith, demonstrating a lack of spiritual maturity in specific areas of life. The Are We There Yet? Fury leaves believers feeling frustrated, unworthy, and discouraged about their spiritual progress. While others are soaring, they only seem to inch along at less than a snail's pace.

Anchors in the Storm

The scriptures teach that God provides a pathway to victory for every trial or temptation we face. Just as there are five Furies that cause the Lost in Faith Experience, there are five key *anchors* that help us overcome them (a different anchor for each Fury). These anchors are firmly secured to the bedrock of eternal truth. They hold fast to the unchanging light of truth, even in times of thickest darkness. Let me briefly introduce each one.

1. *Space Yourself*

The Space Yourself anchor tenet addresses the Processing without Progressing Fury, showing the spiritual keys to effectively managing each occurrence or circumstance as it comes. Spacing Yourself strengthens the bond of trust in our relationship with God and provides a clear guide to keeping life refreshing and moving forward vibrantly, fruitfully, and decisively—regardless of what we have to deal with. By the way, if you think this has anything to do with time management—think again.

2. *Pace Yourself*

The Pace Yourself anchor addresses the Running When You Should Be Walking and Walking When You Should Be Running Fury, teaching the keys to maximizing ourselves from moment to moment. It shows us how to understand God's timetable for our lives and more importantly, how to guarantee we're synchronized with him.

3. *Waste Yourself*

The Waste Yourself anchor addresses the Entrenched in Stench Fury. It shows how to effectively resolve and rid ourselves of the bondage from emotional or mental scars—past or present.

4. *Place Yourself*

The Place Yourself anchor addresses the Assimilation Mutation Fury. This anchor provides key insights into understanding, cultivating, and protecting your personal and spiritual identity, even amidst pressure to conform to standards that everyone else accepts.

5. *Grace Yourself*

Finally, the Grace Yourself anchor addresses the Are We There Yet? Fury, breaking down the four stages of spiritual growth and demystifying the spiritual transformation process—from the beginning wretch-undone starting point all the way to the soaring-on-wings-of-eagles stage.

> Space Yourself.
> Pace Yourself.
> Waste Yourself.
> Place Yourself.
> Grace Yourself.

Not only do these five anchors lay the foundation for recovery from the Lost in Faith Experience, they also help the believer reestablish a pathway forward—a pathway that's both fruitful and rewarding. Learning how to apply any one of these anchors effectively will make a tremendous difference in your life. If you're able to develop all five of them your life will change forever (and have a tremendous positive impact on those around you).

Silent but Deadly

Earlier in this chapter, I said these Furies are five of the deadliest threats to the twenty-first century faith community. I understand that some feel that other more serious problems are pounding harder on the faith community's door. Problems like world hunger, economic collapse, human trafficking, drugs and drug wars, incurable diseases, pornography, the rise of non-essential abortions—the list goes on and on.

I agree that these *are* serious problems and we *should* be concerned with them, but none of them (of themselves) present a *lethal* threat to the faith community. In fact, the faith community has answers for all the problems mentioned above. The message of faith and the power of mercy and grace working through the life of the believer can bring relief and healing to people affected by these social ills. What's more, dealing with these kinds of problems has always been part of our mission—to be salt and light to the world.

Others may point to specific enemies of the faith community as bigger threats. Enemies like post-modernism or legislation aimed at stripping the faith community of its influence, its civic privileges, and even its right to exist.

While serious, this kind of persecution isn't new, and it tends to produce growth in the faith community—not decline. Historically, this kind of pressure has strengthened the faith community's resolve and solidified its will to exist. It forces believers to rely on God with greater intensity, laying aside distractions as they, with one accord, seek God's help in time of trouble.

The furies listed in this book have earned the label of the five deadliest threats to the twenty-first-century faith community for two reasons: the sinister ways they enter our lives, and the quiet, unrelenting devastation they cause once they're there.

These threats appear without notice, like the dust that quietly settles on the floor just beneath the headboard. They find an unguarded place in our soul and blend in with all the other safe material we store.

They are spiritual parasitic infections. Like most parasites, they thrive and throb beneath the surface, becoming disgustingly fat at the expense of their unwitting hosts. We (the faith community) provide housing for these deadly Furies. We nourish and feed them. We even unknowingly infect each other. As Walt Kelly said in his well-known Pogo comic strip, "We have met the enemy, and he is us."

These Five Furies pose a serious threat to every member of the twenty-first-century faith community—without exception. Not only do they infect those we see as fickle and spiritually uncommitted, but they also infect people who've held strong spiritual belief—the ones we consider stalwarts and mainstays of the faith community.

Once established, they methodically work to create millions of tiny leak-points in our souls. They don't use spiritual explosives to blast gaping holes in our belief systems—no, that would attract our attention and we'd respond to it immediately. They don't even try to remove anything important from our spiritual inventory. They just make these tiny, tiny holes that leak ever so slowly, but ever so consistently.

In the meantime we maintain our normal spiritual routines. We keep leading worship and distributing food to the poor. We help with the youth ministry and serve as ushers. We preach on Sundays and teach the midweek Bible classes. We give to missions programs and visit local prisons.

One day, we shake ourselves to rally to some spiritual need, and discover, like Samson, that the familiar stream of spiritual power has become a dusty, dried-out riverbed.

These Furies are poured into the molds of endurance and cast in the furnaces of patience. They are in no hurry. The leaks they cause can go undetected for years, even decades—until it's too late. They work little by little until our virtue tanks can no longer retain what God pours into us.

In the end, they don't cause us to plunge headlong into blatant transgression against God. Instead, they simply deflate us, stealing the bite first, knowing that the bark will die later. They leave us inept and lukewarm . . . fit to be spewed out of the mouth.

I mentioned earlier that 70 percent of people in today's faith community are dissatisfied with their current spiritual experience. Of this group, 90 percent say they have no intention of abandoning their faith. The sad reality, however, is that over 45 percent of this at-risk crowd will, in fact, become casualties of this crisis. Statistics show that they're simply not going to survive.

Let's not deceive ourselves; the demands on the believer in the twenty-first century are more challenging than any preceding age. According to scripture, as the clock for this age winds down we'll see a number of noticeable changes in the world. One such change will be a phenomenon called *The Great Falling Away* (see 2 Thess. 2:3).

The Great Falling Away refers to a sweeping abandonment of faith in God. This defection will be on an unprecedented scale, diminishing the ranks of the faith community throughout the earth. The Five Furies are exactly the kind of threat that can weaken the faith community and lay the groundwork for such a catastrophic event.

In spite of the tremendous damage caused by these Five Furies, the good news is the five anchors presented in this book are even more resilient. They reverse the effects of the Five Furies and bring relief, recovery, and spiritual freedom to believers at an encouraging rate. These tenets are true anchors in light, holding the believer firmly in place against the forces that rage against the twenty-first-century faith community.

My approach in this book is no different than my approach to one-on-one ministry. I realize that people today demand instant answers and even faster results. However, I've learned that when it comes to matters of spiritual health, hasty solutions rarely last. While I appreciate speedy service as much as anyone, I'm much more interested in being effective over the long term than efficient in the short run.

Because of this, my aim isn't writing the shortest book or providing the quickest answer. In some cases, I'm not rushing to get right to the point, because there are simply too many important stones that need turning over along the way. I'm writing this book because I've seen firsthand how its message stops the spiritual bleeding, reverses the trends, and rescues lives from further devastation.

The model has been proven effective. With nothing less than your spiritual wellbeing at stake, the risk is too high to take a lesser approach. I'm interested and invested in *your* long-term spiritual success, health, and welfare—not just in giving you a breather from life's troubles.

One of the ancient books of wisdom instructs us to make gaining understanding a high priority (see Prov. 4:7). It's almost impossible for us to overcome what we don't understand. That's why in each chapter I take the time to analyze these Furies: where do they come from, how do they get established in our lives, and why are they flourishing now?

After that, I present the solutions—and that's not a drive-thru presentation either. God not only wants us to finish our races, but finish them gloriously. When we don't prepare properly we run well, but don't finish strongly . . . *if* we finish.

If you're suffering from any form of the Lost in Faith Experience, here are a set of tools to help you regain vitality and energy in your walk of faith, and move your life forward fruitfully and purposefully. The pathway forward for each person reading this book begins with the very next step. So let's turn the page and begin the journey back to wholeness.

Chapter 2

SPACE
YOURSELF

Rediscovering trust

Take a minute to look over these two illustrations.

Illustration A appears to be some type of newsletter, while Illustration B looks like a bunch of letters squeezed together at the top of a page and dumped on top of a picture.

Now let's look at Illustration A again, this time focusing particularly on the layout. We can see the title, a table of contents, a lead story, some bullet-points of interest, and a second story towards the bottom. There's an interesting picture in the upper section, and some attention-grabbing text in the middle of the page. Everything is separated by lines and borders. Overall it's pretty easy to read.

Now let's get back to Illustration B. It might be a single paragraph or just a string of random letters. The way the text spills over the picture leads us to think that the picture's not supposed to be there, but that's not quite clear either. It's pretty confusing.

Now here's something that might surprise you about these two illustrations. They both contain the *exact same* words, the same text,

Illustration A

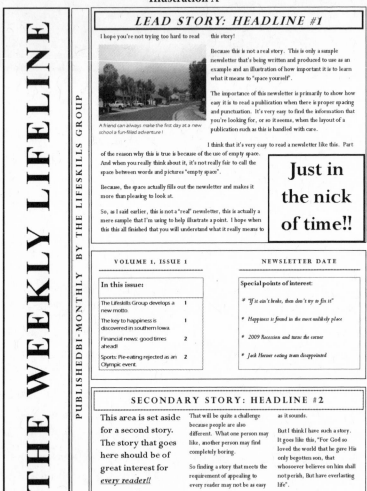

LEAD STORY: HEADLINE #1

I hope you're not trying too hard to read this story!

Because this is not a real story. This is only a sample newsletter that's being written and produced to use as an example and an illustration of how important it is to learn what it means to "space yourself".

The importance of this newsletter is primarily to show how easy it is to read a publication when there is proper spacing and punctuation. It's very easy to find the information that you're looking for, or so it seems, when the layout of a publication such as this is handled with care.

I think that it's very easy to read a newsletter like this. Part of the reason why this is true is because of the use of empty space. And when you really think about it, it's not really fair to call the space between words and pictures "empty space".

Because, the space actually fills out the newsletter and makes it more than pleasing to look at.

So, as I said earlier, this is not a "real" newsletter, this is actually a mere sample that I'm using to help illustrate a point. I hope when this this all finished that you will understand what it really means to

A friend can always make the first day at a new school a fun-filled adventure !

Just in the nick of time!!

VOLUME 1, ISSUE 1

In this issue:

The Lifeskills Group develops a new motto.	1
The key to happiness is discovered in southern Iowa.	1
Financial news: good times ahead!	2
Sports: Pie-eating rejected as an Olympic event.	2

NEWSLETTER DATE

Special points of interest:

* *"If it ain't broke, then don't try to fix it"*

* *Happiness is found in the most unlikely place*

* *2009 Recession and turns the corner*

* *Jack Horner eating team disappointed*

SECONDARY STORY: HEADLINE #2

This area is set aside for a second story. The story that goes here should be of great interest for *every reader!!*

That will be quite a challenge because people are also different. What one person may like, another person may find completely boring.

So finding a story that meets the requirement of appealing to every reader may not be as easy

as it sounds.

But I think I have such a story. It goes like this, "For God so loved the world that he gave His only begotten son, that whosoever believes on him shall not perish, But have everlasting life".

THE WEEKLY LIFELINE

PUBLISHED BI-MONTHLY BY THE LIFESKILLS GROUP

the same picture, and they're on paper the same size. The difference is how the information is laid out on the page.

In Illustration A, the text is formatted differently throughout the document. Each section contains a single topic, punctuation marks are used to help give each story the right tone, and lines and borders keep everything orderly. By contrast, Illustration B looks like a word

Illustration B

the weekly lifeline published bi-monthly by the lifeskills group lead story: headline #1 i hope you're not trying too hard to read this story because this is not a real story this is only a sample newsletter that's being written and produced to use as an example and an illustration of how important it is to learn what it means to "space yourself" the importance of this newsletter is primarily to show how easy it is to read a publication when there is proper spacing and punctuation it's very easy to find the information that you're looking for or so it seems when the layout of a publication such as this is handled with care i think that it's very easy to read a newsletter like this part of the reason why this is true is because of the use of empty space and when you really think about it it's not really fair to call the space between words and pictures "empty space" because, the space actually fills out the newsletter and makes it more than pleasing to look at so, as i said earlier, this is not a "real" newsletter this is actually a mere sample newsletter to help illustrate a point i hope when this this all finished that you will understand what it really means to a friend can a new school a fun-filled adventure just in the nick of time volume 1 issue 1 in this issue: the lifeskills group key to happiness is discovered in southern iowa 1 financial news: good times ahead 2 sports: pie-eating newsletter date special points of interest: "if it ain't broke then don't try to fix it" happiness is found in recession and turns the corner jack horner eating team disappointed secondary story: headline #2 this for a second story the story that goes here should be of great interest for every reader that will be quite a challenge because people are also different what one person may like another person may find completely boring so finding a story that meets the requirement of appealing to every reader may not be as easy as it sounds but i think i have such a story. it goes like this, "for god so loved the world that he gave his only begotten son, that whosoever believes on him shall not perish, but have everlasting life"

processor threw up on top of a picture that happened to be in the wrong place at the wrong time!

There's one other specific difference between these two illustrations—something that's very easily overlooked. Illustration A has spaces—spaces that show us where one word stops and another word starts. Spaces between sentences, separating thoughts and keeping topics from clashing. Spaces between the text and borders, around the picture, and between sections. Spaces that help make sense of everything on the page—spaces that are absent from Illustration B.

As much as anything else, the missing spaces in Illustration B takes what is informative and helpful in one scenario and reduces it to useless gibberish in another.

Processing Without Progressing

Illustration B represents the congested lifestyles that many people in the faith community live today. For many of us life is a series of seemingly unrelenting events, randomly crashing into each other. We try to handle things as they come, but sometimes the way we handle them creates worse problems. In time we feel that things have gotten so out of control that our life has stopped making sense. I call the chronic stage of this condition the Processing without Progressing Fury.

The Processing without Progressing Fury comes on the heels of a pattern of mishandling life's events. It's not that we're completely negligent in handling our affairs; it's just that we often don't handle them appropriately—our actions don't move life forward. Before we know it we've accumulated a pile of partially handled matters. All this unfinished business loiters through the hallways of our minds and weigh on our souls.

Compare this condition to cleaning a cluttered room by stuffing everything into a closet. The goal is to give the room a neat appearance by stashing things out of sight instead of putting them away properly. It's a short-term solution that creates additional work in the long term. Our *intention* is to give the stuff in the closet the proper *attention* later, but as Bruce Bickel and Stan Jantz point out, when intention and attention come together the result is usually failure.[4]

Most of us have thousands of these internal storage closets, each stuffed with thousands of partially processed affairs—like a warehouse full of discarded boxes of partially chewed gourmet chocolates.

The result is a weight on our souls that we know to be real but difficult to pinpoint because it's an accumulation of so many unrelated things. In the end, the sense of burden becomes a lingering part of our daily consciousness.

This "soul weight" drains the spiritual and emotional energy we need to make that day the best day possible. It waits for us to wake up so it can deny us the benefit of feeling rested, even after a full night's sleep. It stretches us out like hot taffy on a Kentucky summer guardrail, producing mental and physical stress—and even leading to serious illness. That's what the Illustration B lifestyle is like.

Illustration A, on the other hand, symbolizes the life of a person who handles the circumstances of life with an understanding of the spiritual anchor I refer to as *Space Yourself.* There's a lot of information on the page—much of it seemingly unrelated—yet it's all still easy to read, easy to understand, and nothing seems out of order or overwhelming.

Space Yourself Defined

So exactly what does it mean to Space Yourself? Spacing Yourself is a way of understanding the interactive component of the relationship between God and man. It helps us see that relationship through the lens of trust—God's definition of trust, not ours.

Spacing Yourself takes us beyond the simple idea that God is trustworthy to a more precise understanding of just why he's worth trusting and gives us practical ways to build that bond of trust. It goes to the fundamental structure of trusting God's way of handling the circumstances of our lives.

The Processing without Progressing Fury is always escorted by F-U-D (Fear-Uncertainty-Doubt). You might be uncertain, for example, about what needs to be done or how best to handle a situation. You might be afraid of missing God's will and making a disastrous choice. Perhaps you doubt your ability or resources to get a job done. Or maybe you're just mentally exhausted—you've reached your limit and you just can't think clearly about one more thing. Spacing Yourself addresses the F-U-D factor head-on, and moves us confidently through the looming shadows of these hindrances.

Spacing Yourself is also about discovering new paths to trusting God. It reinforces the reliability of God's framework for handling situations, knowing they will produce the best results. It also clarifies our legitimate limits and responsibilities in handling our affairs.

Spacing Yourself is the first anchor in recovering from the Lost in Faith Experience. Let's begin by studying God's ways of handling the different circumstances of our lives.

Scripture says, "Let all things be done decently and in order" (1 Cor.14:40). Spacing Yourself clarifies the relationships between *order, space*, and *progress* in managing life's affairs. The scriptures have quite a bit to say about order and confusion in our personal lives, as well as the bond between order and space. We'll never have genuine order without understanding its relationship to space.

Proper "spacing" in life means that we separate things that need separating, isolate things that need isolating, associate things that need association, and that we use the right borders and placement to frame our situations. We don't combine things that we know will produce confusion. Most of all, we include God in our decision-making processes rather than leaning solely on our own understanding.

Spacing Yourself helps us see our realities in true context instead of the out-of-proportion view that the urgency of the moment tries to force on us.

This anchor is as old as creation and can be seen clearly in the book of Genesis in the *Creation Narrative.* The first verse of this passage reads: "In the beginning God created the heavens and the earth" (Gen. 1:1). The word "created" is translated from the Hebrew word *bara,* which primarily means: "to shape; to fashion *existing matter* [italics added] into something new; to transform."

The first verse says God created the world. However, something happened between verse one and verse two that left the earth uninhabitable, literally without form and void. God addressed this problem by "spacing" the world until it was orderly and functional.

If you read the narrative carefully, you'll discover that *most* of what was taking place wasn't a matter of God creating anything new from nothing but rather putting existing elements of the world in their proper space. Look at these examples:

- Genesis 1:4—God separates the *existing* light from the *existing* darkness and puts them both in their proper place.
- Genesis 1:7—God separates the *existing* terrestrial waters from the *existing* atmospheric waters and puts a permanent border (firmament/sky) between them.
- Genesis 1:9–10—Initially, the surface of the earth was completely covered with water; God took that *existing* condition and arranged a balance between the dry land and the sea so that earth's surface now consisted of a perfect balance between the two.

This formless, inhabitable planet was transformed into a world perfectly suited for life—all because God put everything in its proper place. He "spaced" it. In the same way, when it comes to our lives we don't necessarily need new things to make life work, we simply need to learn how to put what we have in proper spatial context.

Spacing Yourself takes this same timeless wisdom and applies it to your life—taking into account these five crucial factors:

1. The different roles we each have (i.e., mother, wife, daughter, friend, employer, etc.)
2. The natural course of each occurrence we're dealing with (i.e. an illness, a promotion at work, a contentious relationship, a financial emergency, etc.)
3. A sensitivity to others who may be involved or affected by the way we handle the situation
4. An understanding of the existence of spiritual realities—unseen forces—that can influence our situation positively or negatively
5. Unwavering confidence that God wants our circumstances to work for his divine purposes and our ultimate well-being. To that end, we can know confidently that God's intervening assistance is available to help us.

Space Yourself 101

Spacing Yourself is about order—but not necessarily sequential order (or even a FIFO-LIFO list). It's an exercise in godly order—which goes beyond the catchphrase to "always put God first."

Like pieces on a chessboard, everything in our lives has a proper place and an appropriate path for directional movement. In chess, no two pieces can ever occupy the same square. Each piece is also limited in how it can move on the board. For example, the "bishops" can only move diagonally on either exclusively black or white squares. The "rooks" can only move vertically or horizontally. The "pawns" are the only pieces that aren't allowed to move backwards.

No one is born knowing the rules and movements of chess—they learn about these things somewhere along the path of life. In the same way, it's up to us to learn the proper place and the paths for the elements in our lives. What's the appropriate way to express anger? What about laughter? How far should we allow grieving to go on when we lose a loved one? What should our course of action be when our backs are against the wall and we have no idea what to do next?

Is there ever a place for hatred in our lives? When does personal ambition cross the line? The Bible mentions that God is a jealous God—does that mean it's okay for us to be jealous? Exactly how do we love people who are trying to ruin our lives? Spacing Yourself provides a guideline and anchor for addressing these kinds of questions and keeping life on track.

Think of your life as your own "personal galaxy." Now think of the people, places, and circumstances of your life as planets, moons, and stars. In order to co-exist harmoniously everything has to stay in its proper orbit and assigned place. Each part of our situation (including each thought, expression, and action) has its own unique qualities and proper place in the scheme of our lives; and each part is designed to run on a specific track within our personal world. When out of place, things that are meant to be part of a harmonious co-existence suddenly become dangerous asteroids that threaten to disrupt everything in our galaxy.

Everything we deal with has a proper place in our lives—even the things that seem distasteful. As new things come into our lives, it's up to us to make sure that they're put in the right space. We also see to it that existing matters don't get pushed out of place. As long as everything is in its proper space and running on the right course, our lives will stay "on track."

Staying on track doesn't mean we won't have difficult days or tough seasons. That's where trusting God is the hardest but matters most—when we do the right thing for the right reason and still end up in a pit. That's why the apostle Paul, who could have written an entire thesis on "The Highs and Lows of Living by Faith," could say: "That's why we can be so sure that every detail in our lives of love for God is worked into something good" (Rom. 8:28 MSG).

No matter how bad things may look presently, when put on God's prescribed "track," these events will settle into a trajectory that has a positive ending. However, when we ignore the proper course and formation of our circumstances we can easily wind up in a state of confusion.

For example, suppose a married woman is having lunch with a male co-worker and she begins to share some personal problems she and her husband are having. The male co-worker is receptive, understanding, and supportive—at this point, he's just trying to be a good friend. She appreciates the supportive conversation— perhaps something she doesn't get from her husband.

These lunchbox sharing sessions become routine and the topics soon expand to other areas of their lives. Before long, they're both looking forward to having lunch together. They may see it as merely a refreshing break from a tedious workday or a chance to talk about the things they enjoy in life with someone they like being around.

Over the course of time, however, they subconsciously develop emotional bonds that teeter precariously close to the edge of a dating relationship. By this time, the proper paths for the roles of wife, co-worker, and friend have already been violated. It's just a matter of time before there's a more obvious expression of this violation—a violation which, in many cases, is brought about through the manipulation of circumstances by unseen spiritual forces working in the spaces around us (I don't blame every calamity on evil spiritual forces, but in some cases, they're a factor).

Spacing Yourself allows you to maintain order in your life through it all. It keeps you from being overwhelmed by life's happenings.

Many of you know what it's like to be *so* drained from dealing with just *one* ongoing problem in your life; by day's end you have no emotional, mental, or physical energy left.

You can push back effectively by learning to Space Yourself.

Spacing Yourself also shows us how to understand and master the boundaries of our own attitudes and actions when dealing with our situations. When we learn how to properly space ourselves we become better stewards of our lives. The result is a life that steadily moves forward vibrantly, decisively, and fruitfully.

Space Yourself 201

The process of Spacing Yourself includes five foundational sub-tenets that can't be ignored. All five apply to each situation we face.

Gravity Matters: Each event of life—whether good or bad—has a certain "weight" or "mass" to it. This "weight" will tug at our souls and pull us towards it—in the same way that gravity pulls on physical objects. If we give in to this type of circumstantial magnetism, then we'll allow our circumstances to drastically alter the order of our lives by "pulling" us out of our natural orbit. That's how people become obsessed with things they experience in life—their lives literally began to revolve around a particular event that demands their attention. If you can imagine the disastrous consequences to the universe if the sun suddenly started rotating around the earth, then you get the picture. Whether circumstances are good or bad, you've been designed to transcend them, not to be manipulated or controlled by them.

Role, Role, Role Your Boat: Secondly, it's important to identify the role that relates to what you're dealing with. For example, I'm a husband, a father, a brother, a son, a friend, a nephew, a cousin, an uncle, a pastor, and a teacher. If one of my sons comes up to me and tells me about a problem he's having, is he looking for a fatherly ear or pastoral counsel? My response as a pastor is different from my response as a father. Even though these roles can be assigned to the same person, their paths have two very different endpoints and will most likely require very different responses.

Spacing Yourself helps us recognize the purposes of and boundaries for the different roles we serve; it also helps us associate what we're dealing with to the appropriate role—and subsequently the right track. One memorable example of this comes from the historical account of King David's rise to the throne. When David was made king over Israel, he was escorted into the royal city by over 340,000 soldiers from the twelve tribes of Israel. The historian pays special attention, however, to two hundred leaders from the tribe of Issachar, who were described as men who understood the times and knew exactly what Israel should do (see 1 Chron. 12:32). Doing the right thing at the right time for the right reason is one of the major keys to keeping life moving forward vibrantly, fruitfully, and decisively.

As Time Goes By: Thirdly, we must understand that circumstances, no matter how final they seem, are temporary. Whether a situation is considered good, bad, or indifferent, we should remember that the particular situation (including its problems, ramifications, our feelings about what's happening, etc.) won't remain that way. Think of it this way: no matter how dark the night may be, it will eventually be replaced by daylight. It really doesn't make sense to stay up worrying or praying for the daylight to come—it's coming regardless of what we do. Perhaps a better use of our time and energy would be in developing patience, understanding, or vision-casting.

The point to remember is most things change as a matter of *design*. As Bernard Ighner wrote in his classic song, *Everything Must Change*, "'Cause that's the way of time, nothing and no one goes unchanged."[5] Of course, this means that in the short term things could get better or things could get worse; but one thing's for sure:

things won't stay the same. Understanding the stage of our circumstances helps us to know the best way to respond. When you learn how to Space Yourself you're positioning yourself properly for whatever develops—bringing to bear the patience and thinking needed to move forward wisely.

Like Water off a Duck's Back: Fourthly, we must understand that while the particular event may have become part of our environment it's not part of us. For example, you may have worked hard on your job and earned a great promotion. Or you could have worked just as hard only to be fired because of someone else's incompetence or dishonesty. Whatever the case, don't let a permanent bond develop between what you do, the events that happen to you, and *who* you are. If you do, you'll only end up with a distorted view of both yourself and the world around you.

For example, as a child, I remember hearing a story about the donkey that Jesus rode when he entered the city of Jerusalem. If you recall, all the people were shouting "Hosanna" and laying palm branches on the ground as Jesus passed by. Later that evening the donkey was in the stable with the other animals. He bragged about how the crowd was so impressed with *his* excellent trotting style that they honored *him* by laying palm branches on the ground for *him* to walk on!

The other barnyard animals were eating up every word the donkey said and began to offer him gifts of food—they figured if everyone else thought he was that special, then they needed to jump on the same bandwagon! This donkey had a false impression of himself (to say the least), and the other animals in the barnyard community were gullible enough to go along with him. Their lives were turned topsy-turvy—all because they embraced the misunderstandings of one misguided creature. I believe Rudyard Kipling hit the nail on the head when he wrote,

> If you can meet with Triumph and Disaster
> And treat those two impostors just the same. . . .[6]

As you understand how to Space Yourself in each situation, you'll mature in your ability to keep your eyes on the true prize at all times, reducing the possibility of developing a false sense of grandeur, a skewed sense of entitlement, a poverty mindset, or a victim mentality.

The Himpossible Factor: Fifthly, we must remember that no matter how severe or incurable our current circumstances may seem, when we make room (space) for God to operate on our behalf, *nothing remains impossible for long.*

Muhammed Ali once said, "Impossible is only temporary." The Space Yourself anchor changes "impossible's" status. By acknowledging God's terms of order the impossible forcibly becomes *Himpossible.* We take our impossible circumstances and respond to them God's way. With God, *nothing* is impossible. Through our faith, our trust, and our wisdom-based actions, we can ignite the process that transforms *any* situation.

For example, one minute the patriarch Joseph is wasting away in prison on trumped up rape charges, and a few days later he's the governor of Egypt (see Gen. 40–41). No doubt, Joseph would have been satisfied just to be out of prison, but God's ultimate plan always exceeds what we would gladly merely settle for.

The flipside to this truth is this: no matter how wonderful or perfect our current circumstances may seem, *when we fail to honor godly order, nothing good remains possible.* The "Himpossible" converts back to an overwhelming difficulty when "space" is missing. Through our failure to acknowledge God's place in our circumstances, we can leave the door cracked to forfeit the good things we have. Without the right space, what was a miraculous possibility quickly reverts to an impossibility.

By the way, acknowledging God isn't just mental assent to his existence. At minimum, it means that we know, honor, and submit to the specific things that the scriptures teach about our kind of circumstance. For example if someone mistreats you, the scriptures clearly teach us not to seek revenge or repay those who have wronged us with equal harm (see Rom. 12:17, 19). In view of this passage, acknowledging God in this situation would mean that you don't try to retaliate.

When we apply the anchor of Spacing Yourself, we not only bring the transforming power of God to bear in every situation, but we also establish the proper attitude about the situation. This helps us not to misinterpret what's actually happening (and as a result handle it improperly).

Space Yourself 301

Earlier in the chapter, I gave an example of the rules of movement for the game of chess. Here are ten guidelines to help you decide the right "moves" when handling any circumstance. It's important to commit these to memory (through prayer, meditation, and worship) and factor them into your decision-making process. They will apply the Space Yourself anchor to your situation so that you can move your circumstances forward with purpose.

1. Things that appear distressing could actually contain great blessing (see Gen. 50:20).
2. Things that appear to be a blessing could actually conceal devastating complications (see Gen. 16:1–5).
3. The ultimate outcome of each occurrence can only be appreciated in retrospect (see Job 42:3), so don't make presumptions about your circumstances at the beginning or while you're still in the middle of them.

4. The "spiritual space" between you and your occurrence will eventually be occupied by unseen forces that will work for your good, work against you, or operate indifferent to you (see 2 Kgs. 6:16–17; Josh. 5:13–14; Eph. 6:12).

5. You have considerable authority regarding the activities of the spiritual entities that fill the immaterial space around you. In fact, in most cases, it's your behavior—your decisions—that control this behind-the-scenes activity. Turn on the spiritual fire hose and flood the environment with words, thoughts, and actions that correspond to what you already know the scriptures teach about your situation and the outcome you desire.

6. Remember that God always has you in his mind, and because of that, only allows things to come into your life that ultimately will be of use to his good plan for you (see Ps. 40:5, Jer. 29:11), and that you can overcome.

7. Both happiness and sadness are unavoidable event-driven realities of living. Recognize that these feelings can be produced artificially (for example by watching a movie that's completely fictional) and are not reliable compasses. We can experience and express these feelings safely, as long as we filter them through the unchangeable joy that's a gift from God (a spiritual—not emotional—reality). This type of joy is an anchor-pin that prevents us from giving in to the pressures of the sense of urgency connected to our situations—a sense often amplified by feelings of happiness or sadness.

8. You may feel isolated—but you're never completely alone (see Deut. 31:8).

9. Spacing Yourself isn't always about resolving every situation to your liking, at least not initially. Some things are going to

work out in ways you don't care for at the time. It's important that you don't let this throw you off track—keep your commitment to do the right thing at the right time for the right reasons (see 1 Cor. 15:58).

10. Don't lose sight of one crucial element of God's plan for his children—that our lives are meant to glorify God and draw others to him by witnessing to them through what they see in us. God has brought you forth at this time and placed you in your particular cultural setting so that (through you) God can speak to others in ways they can relate to. The way you handle different situations may be the only "gospel" message that some people ever see (see 2 Cor. 3:2–3).

The ability to Space Yourself is embedded in our faith. It's part of our nature, a part that has to be intentionally developed. Spacing Yourself will help keep you from being overwhelmed mentally, exhausted emotionally, or blinded spiritually. It simultaneously helps build your physical health, your relationships, and your dreams. No matter how impossible or convoluted a situation may seem, amazingly, the answers began to materialize as you learn to Space Yourself.

As you're reading this, you may be thinking about how this can help your spouse, child, sibling, cousin, friend, co-worker, or in-law. Here's my advice; you can always buy a copy of the book and give it to them later...but for now, let's *not* think about them. There's a specific reason that the anchor is called Space *Yourself.* This anchor is about you and for you—not someone else.

Stop living other people's lives for a minute and focus on your own. Start applying what you've learned to your own life. Don't fall into the deception that because you've read it and understood it, you're benefiting from it (that might not be the case). I'm praying that you don't turn out like the man in Jesus' parable who heard the word, immediately received it with gladness, and then, because he had no root in himself, only endured for a time (see Mk 4:16–17).

I close this chapter with an excerpt from a poem I wrote as a tribute to my grandmother when she died. She had very little formal education, but was one of the wisest, most intelligent and amazing people I've ever known. This stanza puts the Space Yourself anchor in the right perspective:

> *Life is made up of many things,*
> *Your past, your present, and your dreams,*
> *And each one has its perfect place,*
> *Its time, its order, rank, and space.*[7]

Chapter 3

S-O-S

Ten keys to thriving in the storm

Spacing Yourself requires us to make decisions that maintain, restore, or create spiritual order in our lives. It would be great if we could develop this tenet at our own pace in a peaceful, controlled learning environment—but don't count on it. Most of us are going to learn these principles as we go through life's storms. Don't panic; this chapter presents lessons that are particularly suited for "on the job training."

Most of our problems are outcomes of our habits. We'll need to change many of these habits, particularly those that are secular (no matter how popular). When I use the word "secular," I'm referring to any thought process, attitude, or course of action that doesn't recognize God as the preeminent factor.

Changing habits is rarely easy, but it's do-able. More importantly, it's worth the effort.

I've put together a list of ten practical steps that will help you learn to replace harmful habits with new routines that put the Space Yourself anchor to work for you. I call them the *Ten S-O-S's*.

What exactly does the term S-O-S mean? You can probably relate to trying to get settled in your seat at a theater or on a church pew when an usher comes along and asks everyone to "scoot over some" in order to make room for a newcomer. I've also heard that same phrase ("scoot over some") coming from the back seat of our car when our three kids were trying to get a little bit more elbow room.

"Scoot over some" is simply a way of recognizing that new demands are being put on existing space. The acronym for the phrase "scoot over some" is "S-O-S," which also happens to be the Morse code signal for "HELP!" I like the marriage of the two ideas.

Sometimes we need an S-O-S because the events of our lives are starting to squeeze us, crowd us, and restrict our freedom of movement or thought. Sometimes we need an S-O-S in order to make room for God and the resources he wants to bring into our situation. In either case, the S-O-S acronym fits well with the Space Yourself precept.

Here's the list:

S-O-S #1: Immediately put God in the space between you and your situation.

The moment you find yourself in a new situation—good or bad— immediately put God and his resources between you and that situation. No matter how insignificant the task may seem, don't try to handle it directly or independently. Create some distance between you and the issue and maintain a safe cushion. Space Yourself.

Here's an illustration to help you get a picture of what the spatial order in this process should look like:

Don't let yourself come into direct contact with the situation you're dealing with. Compare it to the relationship between the kneecap and the knee bones. There are ligaments, tissue, and fluid between the kneecap and the knee bones. These provide a cushion

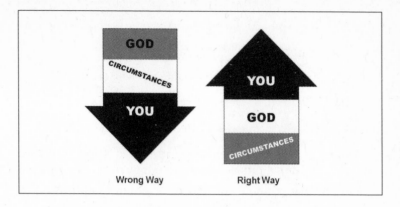

between the bones, making it possible for a person to move about freely without pain. They also aid in supporting a person's weight or any additional weight that the person may need to carry. However, when the material between the kneecap and the knee bone becomes damaged or begins to wear away, the bones come in direct contact with each other. Without the cushion, the bones grind against each other, causing excruciating pain and making movement difficult.

In the same way, when you learn to Space Yourself, you put the proper cushion between you and your situation, making it possible to continue moving about freely without being burdened down by the weight of what you're dealing with. Without this cushion, your situation will grind and grate you into depression, confusion, fear, or some other state of brokenness—limiting your ability to move forward.

Here are a few Bible passages that highlight this anchor:

The Lord your God, *who goes before you* [emphasis added], He will fight for you (Deut. 1:30).

Notice the position that God takes. He goes *before* you (or *in front* of you), occupying the space *between* you and your challenges. God's place should be *between* you and your problem. As long as he's invited between you and the problem, then the problem will never have complete access to you and won't overwhelm you.

> For You, O Lord, will bless the righteous; with favor *You will surround him* as with a shield. (Ps. 5:12)

This passage shows that God wants to fill the spiritual space around us—*with favor*. Favor is a spiritual force that people commonly refer to as "luck." Favor is God's power *forcing* our circumstances to produce results that promote our well-being. No matter what comes against us, favor causes things to eventually work for our good.

The key lies in actively giving place to God and inviting him into our situation *every time*—without exception. Otherwise, for someone who's omnipresent, God can be the most inconspicuous person that we'll ever (or never) encounter.

Finally, listen to King David's thoughts about the matter:

> I have set the Lord always before me; Because He is at my right hand I shall not be moved (Ps. 5:12).

David understood that even though God was with him at all times (at my right hand), the act to "set the Lord always before him" was required to release heaven's resources on his behalf. It was also his responsibility. The same applies to us today. Here's a simple prayer to help you activate this S-O-S:

> *Heavenly Father, regarding (insert the specific situation you're dealing with), I invite you right now to go before me— to surround me—with your abiding Spirit and heavenly resources. I refuse to try to work through this situation solely relying on my own abilities—no matter how uncomplicated it seems. I thank You that right now You're standing between me and the situation I'm facing, and I know that You*

guarantee an outcome that'll be for my good. I'm thankful
for this privilege to come to you in this way . . . a privilege
made possible by the sacrifice of Your Son, Jesus Christ, and
it's in his name that I come to you now.

S-O-S #2: Have a personal conversation with God about the matter, and let him know exactly what you think about it.

I believe that one of the more unfortunate developments among people of faith today is the idea that we have to hide our true feelings (about the things we're dealing with) from God. I've heard entire sermons insisting that we should never express any hint of unbelief, doubt, or fear when we're praying to God. My response is, why not? If I can't tell God what I'm upset with, afraid of, angry about, or uncertain of, then to whom can I express those feelings?

In the first place, God already knows every thought that we think before we think it. He already knows every word that we're going to say before we speak (see Ps. 139:2–4). The unspoken profanities, ponderings over punching someone, and other destructive thoughts we entertain—God already hears them. Keeping our mouths shut doesn't hide any of our thoughts from him—and, by the way, the issue isn't with our mouths so much as it is with our hearts (the mouth draws from the heart). Our words, no matter how outrageous, don't surprise God.

There are times when you are troubled and need to vent. Sometimes you need to open the windows of your soul and air things out. These are times to be candid with God about your thoughts and feelings. It's much better to vent your unfiltered fears and frustrations to God than to dump them on people.

Even while hanging on the cross, Jesus asked what appears to be an unthinkable question when he raised his voice in this heart-wrenching cry, "My God, my God, why have You forsaken me?"

It's as if his humanity burst through all of the prophetic and messianic proceedings, hit the pause button and screamed, "Hey! Exactly what in the world is going on here?!? Father, . . .can you explain to me just why you're abandoning me now—now when I need you the most?" Coming from Emmanuel, that cry is still hard bone and gristle to our theological digestive system. But notice that Jesus' statement didn't even cause the slightest trace of disappointment, surprise, or disapproval from our heavenly Father.

God doesn't get offended. He won't misinterpret words we speak in frustration. He won't gossip about us behind our backs. In the twinkling of an eye, he can erase and repair any damage that might come from something we say. However, we can say the wrong thing at the wrong time to certain people and never be able to repair the damage to the relationship in this life (not that God's mercy isn't enough to repair it, but our carnal, immature minds prevent us from extending his mercy to others or receiving it from them).

Over the years, I've said a lot of things before God that I'm not proud of, and I've made a lot of immature statements in prayer that I've had to repent of and ask forgiveness for later. Sometimes, just hearing myself say certain things helped me realize how foolish, carnal, and childish those feelings were. Thankfully, in each case God always used my own statements as part of my learning experience. He never leveled any additional penalty against me for speaking what was on my mind, no matter how selfish, ungodly, or off-centered it really was.

Here's a simple prayer to help you put this S-O-S into practice:

Dear Lord, I thank you for loving me enough to listen to what I'm feeling about this situation. Your word reminds me that Your ears are open to my cries (Ps. 34:15). Here's how I feel about what I'm facing right now: (express your feelings and thoughts specifically; remember to cover all the bases!). I commit my thoughts and feelings to You and I ask You to cause my outlook to harmonize perfectly with how You want me to think and feel about this circumstance (see Prov. 16:3 AMP). *I'm grateful for the privilege to come to you in this way, a privilege made possible by the sacrifice of Your Son, Jesus Christ, and it's in his name that I come to you now* (see Jn. 16:23–24).

S-O-S #3: Ask God to let you know what he thinks about your situation.

Once you've told God how you feel about your situation, give him an opportunity to tell you how he feels about the same situation. God's general position on virtually anything that happens in life can be found in the Bible, but you need to know how he specifically wants you to handle your situation.

You need wisdom directly from the throne. Remember, each occurrence in your life is unique—no matter how closely it resembles something you've experienced before. You'll make a huge mistake by overlooking this step.

Take the story of the battle of Ai as an example. The people of Israel were coming off a stunning and improbable victory over the walled city of Jericho. Their victory came from the most unconventional battle-plan in the history of warfare. Confidence was at an all-time high throughout the camp as they came upon the next city to be conquered, the city of Ai. As they approached this small town, there wasn't a single doubt throughout the entire group that they would be victorious. With this background in mind, let's take a look at the biblical account of what happened next:

> 2 Now Joshua sent men from Jericho to Ai, which is beside Beth Aven, on the east side of Bethel, and spoke to them,

saying, "Go up and spy out the country." So the men went up and spied out Ai.

³ And they returned to Joshua and said to him, "Do not let all the people go up, but let about two or three thousand men go up and attack Ai. Do not weary all the people there, for the people of Ai are few."

⁴ So about three thousand men went up there from the people, but they fled before the men of Ai.

⁵ And the men of Ai struck down about thirty-six men, for they chased them from before the gate as far as Shebarim, and struck them down on the descent; therefore the hearts of the people melted and became like water.

⁶ Then Joshua tore his clothes, and fell to the earth on his face before the ark of the LORD until evening, he and the elders of Israel; and they put dust on their heads (Josh 7:2–6).

The similarities between the battle preparations for the two skirmishes are striking. In both cases, Joshua sent spies into the land. In both cases, the spies returned with information about the city's weaknesses and strengths. In both cases, the spies offered their advice on how to defeat the enemy. That's where the similarities end and one big difference sticks out.

Before the battle at Jericho, Joshua sought specific direction from God regarding the fight. He presented all of the information that had been gathered, along with all the advice that his generals had offered, and then *asked God for his input* on what they should do and how they should proceed. He didn't assume anything. In contrast, in the case of Ai, Joshua just took the spies' advice and sent in the troops. The result? A defeat as stunning as their previous victory.

To put this in perspective, Ai's defeat of the Israelites would be comparable to a Pop Warner Junior Pee Wee team beating the Green Bay Packers. Couldn't happen in a million years—but the impossible happened. All because they *presumed* to know what God was thinking, rather than simply ask him.

No matter how long you've been walking with God and no matter what your role or title, don't make the mistake of thinking you know *specifically* what God wants to do in any new situation. Ask, seek, and knock . . . until he shares his wisdom with you.

Diana Robinson said, "Prayer is *talking* to God. Meditation is *listening* to God." Here's a simple prayer to help you put this S-O-S into practice:

> *Dear Lord, your word reminds me that when I ask, seek, or knock, you'll hear me and reply. I want to know what your thoughts are regarding the circumstance I'm facing. Please open up my understanding so I can see and hear your exact outlook on this situation. I know you'll speak to me in a way that I can understand what you want me to know. I 'm so thankful for this privilege to come to you in this way, a privilege made possible by the sacrifice of Your Son, Jesus Christ, and it's in his name that I ask these things.*

S-O-S #4: Ask God to guard you against "heart attacks."

The heart—or soul—is the main part of our nature that comes under attack when we decide to exercise our faith. This is because the soul—home to our five senses—is where these decisions are settled (as well as unsettled). The umpires for these decisions (our will, intellect, memories, and emotions—see Appendix A) also reside in the soul.

It takes a while for us to learn how to harmonize faith and flesh or spirit and soul. Even after we've matured in this discipline, we'll still find ourselves conflicted at times. The temptations to abandon our faith and return to a soul-dominated life will come loud and often. Yielding to these temptations puts our spiritual progress in jeopardy—like taking two steps forward and three steps back. That's why the scriptures urge us to practice the daily discipline of walking by faith—learning to lean on our faith senses and not just our natural senses (see 2 Cor. 5:7).

The landlords of our souls (hearts) are highly resistant to the authenticity of spiritual information—of any kind. For most of our lives we've made decisions using our five senses, intellect, memories, and emotions. Now we're adding our sense of faith to the decision-making process. This is a game changer.

It's not that we don't want to incorporate our sense of faith into the decision making process; it's just that the "root system" of our existing decision-making process is deeper and more complicated than we could ever understand. It can be changed, but it won't happen quickly or easily.

Look at what the Bible says about this default decision-making root system: "The heart *is* deceitful above all *things*, and desperately wicked; who can know it?" (Jer. 17:9)

The word "heart" (Hebrew—*lēb*) in this verse is actually referring to the "soul." This passage is not simply identifying the heart (or soul) as a place of inherent evil, but is pointing out that it's so complicated that it's beyond our ability to completely understand.

The word "wicked" in the verse is the perfect word to describe the complex nature of the heart (or soul). The word "wicked" comes from the same root word that gives us the word "wicker" (which is a basket or furniture made of twisted, woven fiber) and "Wicca" (which is the pagan religion of sorcery that twists together various beliefs from the occult, nature, herbal knowledge, and magic). To say that the heart is wicked is to accurately describe the soul as a place of complexly intertwined components which generally lean towards the secular.

The good news is that God knows the precise beginning and end of each strand of what often appears to be a hopelessly tangled mess. He's promised and has proven that not only can he untangle our messes, but he's also more than able to guard our hearts against attacks that come to confuse, disorient, discourage, or distract us when we make the decision to put our faith senses into action (see Phil. 4:7).

Here's a basic prayer that will help you put this S-O-S into practice:

Dear Heavenly Father, as I walk through the circumstance I'm facing right now, please keep and guard my heart against anything that would motivate me to behave or think in ways that work against what's best in this situation. Give me a sound spirit and a bridled tongue. Don't let me be deceived, but let me clearly see the right and good path that you've made for me, even if it comes with hardship. In Jesus' name I pray, amen.

S-O-S #5: Seek a scriptural anchor to stabilize you.

Ask God to give you a specific passage from the Bible that will support what he's trying to do in your life through your situation. This passage will serve as an invaluable anchor, keeping you stable when the winds of adversity and uncertainty come against you.

It's important to remember that this process is spiritual in nature, and any accomplishments that are of a spiritual nature have to be undergirded by spiritual means—the *right* spiritual means. The Bible contains the words and absolute truths that should serve as our "blueprint" for living, and within that blueprint we find the basis for spiritual stability—God's Holy Word. Among other things, God's Word is meant to sustain our efforts to bring spiritual realities into focus.

A great example of this is in Matthew where we read about the account of Jesus' temptation in the wilderness (Matt. 4:1–11). Jesus was alone in a deserted region preparing for his public ministry. During this time he was harassed with various attacks intended to discourage, distract, and tempt him to forfeit his mission.

While the Bible tells us that these temptations came from Satan, there's no indication that Satan was actually physically there with Jesus. It could well be that these temptations were intense thoughts or lingering questions sent by Satan to barrage Jesus' mind. That's the same way he comes against most of us today—with a barrage of thoughts sent to unsettle our faith. In any case, Jesus was able to resist the temptations because he had a specific promise from the Word of God for every temptation he faced.

Here's a prayer to help you put this S-O-S into action:

Heavenly father, I ask that you give me the word that will be a compass for me in this situation—a light to my path and a lamp to my feet. Anchor me in your truth as I walk with you through this situation. I thank you that you hear me, and I know that the deposit of your word will sustain me, strengthen me, and give me clear direction. I pray this in Jesus' name, amen.

S-O-S #6: Acknowledge and depreciate your limitations.

In his 1994 inaugural speech, Nelson Mandela said, "Our deepest fear is not that we are inadequate. Our deepest fear is that we are powerful beyond measure."

The belief that we're powerful beyond measure isn't our deepest fear—it's our grandest delusion. The reality is that each of us will face situations in which the word "can't" applies to us and, in spite of our most noble efforts, will stick to us like chewing gum on hot asphalt. No matter what level of ability, skill, or faith we have, some challenges we just can't overcome on our own.

In many cases our efforts are blocked by a limitation or a weakness—it's important that we understand the difference between the two because they have to be handled differently. Limitations affect the kind of choices available to resolve a problem. Weaknesses, on the other hand, are damaged areas of our lives that invariably force failure upon us—even when we have all the makings for success.

For example certain owls have poor vision in bright sunlight (a limitation) but compensate for this by hunting at night. A weakness would be if an owl had a broken wing, in which case it couldn't hunt at all. Limitations slow us down, but don't normally stop us altogether. Weaknesses, on the other hand, can extinguish the opportunities that come to us.

Limitations pose potential danger to each of us. If they aren't addressed effectively, we usually come up with compromises (substandard solutions) that we use as substitutes for the best (and right) way of doing things. These substandard solutions usually make things worse, not better.

I once saw an illustration of a pioneer-style wagon that had square wheels. The wagon was making plodding, irregular progress, thanks to the sweat and effort of several husky men who were pushing it up the road. However, the most striking feature of the illustration was the contents of the wagon: it was filled with sturdy round wagon wheels!

It's safe to assume that if the men would simply replace the square wheels with the round ones, they'd be able to move along a lot faster and with a lot less effort. They didn't want to stop and change the wheels, however, because no matter how impractical the whole thing seemed, the fact was *the cart was still moving forward*—which was enough for them!

In too many cases as long as there's movement—no matter how slight or painstaking—we tend to accept it, happy to see any progress at all. We accept it and keep going. We often take the path of least resistance—no matter how mediocre. But the gutters of this path are littered with second-rate remedies that break down and give out at the most inconvenient time.

Mediocrity, like a scalp disease, works its way into our souls, attacking the healthy cells of expectation and hope. Eventually we accept this patchiness as a normal part of life. Don't ever accept this; it's a deadly poison to your potential.

The Bible addresses this issue when it tells us: "Thorns and snares are in the way of the perverse; He who guards his soul will be far from them" (Prov. 22:5).

We've got to be vigilant in remembering that these short-term, mediocre remedies will never satisfy the long-range demands of life. Whatever benefit we gain in the short run will be offset by our losses in the end.

Here's the most important thing to remember about limitations: whenever we find ourselves in a situation that can't be resolved (because of our limitations), it's usually a sign that God wants to broaden, deepen, and enrich our lives through change. He wants to show us how he can orchestrate resources and people to help us move our lives forward vibrantly, fruitfully, and decisively.

Voltaire once said, "The good is the enemy of the best." I tend to agree with the general idea, but with this one exception: I wouldn't ever describe the mediocre solutions we come up with as "good."

When we fail to see limitations as part of a change process, we can become stuck in the tar of mediocrity mixed with compromise. Seeing our limitations as part of a change process will help us move to something better. In many cases, God shows us *new ways* where previously there were *no ways*.

Here's a prayer that can help bring this S-O-S to bear in your situation:

> *Heavenly Father, I thank you for the gifts and talents that you've blessed me with. But I admit that these haven't been designed for do-it-yourself or stand-alone living. I admit that I can't succeed relying on my own strengths—even if it appears that they're sufficient for the need at hand. Help me to know my boundaries in this situation and please add what's needed to what I already have so that the best outcome for this situation can be brought about. In Jesus' name, I ask these things, amen.*

S-O-S #7: Acknowledge and appreciate God's strengths.

Volumes have been written about God's unlimited power, an attribute referred to as *omnipotence*. Sometimes these references make us smile, like the time C. S. Lewis said, "A man can no more diminish God's glory by refusing to worship him than a lunatic can put out the sun by scribbling the word, 'darkness' on the walls of his padded cell."

At other times, they make us reflect deeply, as when Charles Blake observed, "If all the oceans of the world were ink and if all the skies were one unfolding scroll, to write about the love of God would soon drain the oceans dry and fill every inch of the skies. . . ."

Within the faith community there's little debate about God's unlimited power. Look at the following passage: "Lord God! Behold, You have made the heavens and the earth by Your great power and by Your outstretched arm! There is nothing too hard *or* too wonderful for You" (Jer. 32:17 AMP).

Even with such a clear declaration of God's power, the chaos we see in the world and our personal circumstances can leave us thinking that maybe God isn't as powerful as his reputation suggests. The questions are all too familiar, "If God is so powerful, why doesn't he do a better job of running things? Why does he allow his plans to be so easily interrupted, and why does he allow so much trouble and suffering?"

There appears to be an arbitrary element to God's power that confuses us, which in turn causes us to look at our challenges with hesitancy. For example, God's choice to heal one person while allowing another person to die from the same sickness. We want to serve a God who does the exact same thing every time—not one who leaves us in limbo.

We believe that he's able—but will he? Will he heal the cancer? Will he keep the marriage from ending? Will he bring that wayward child back home? Will he help our loved one who's struggling with addiction to pornography, or drugs, or an eating disorder? And, the number one question, "Will God come through *this time* for *me*?"

It's important to remember that God's will only appears to be arbitrary; our circumstance is the Rosetta Stone for interpreting his will. God will do exactly what he's said he'll do in his Word. His will, however, is often accomplished through his purpose—which uses sufferings as well as blessings that come into our lives. God exchanges the troubles of our brief, earthly lifespan with eternal blessings in the nearby hereafter. He can do that because he's omnipotent.

It's great to know that God's in control, but there are a lot of times that my circumstances don't seem to support that. For these times, I'd like to give you three keys to help you keep God's ability in proper perspective.

1. Settle in your mind that God has absolute power to fix whatever difficulty you face. The answer to your problem may be somewhere outside your scope of awareness—but not outside God's. Don't doubt his "able-ness"—not even for a second.

2. God's ability is released in accordance to our faith, but don't make the mistake of thinking your faith will be activated by the mere knowledge that God *is* all-powerful. Many believers fall into this trap and end up shipwrecked and disappointed. Remember faith only *comes* by hearing; it is *released and activated* by our intentional, decisive actions.

3. Remember that faith operates by love. The reason that you can expect God to use his power on your behalf is based on the love that he's declared and already demonstrated for you. His love keeps him poised to move on your behalf, even if it means providing a miracle to rescue you from your own fiery furnace experience.

How deep is God's commitment and love for you? Look at the following passage: "He who did not spare His own Son, but delivered Him up for us all, how shall he not with Him also freely give us all things?" (Rom. 8:32). This verse makes it clear that God's love for us was so intense that when he saw mankind held in the grip of deterioration he turned, reached for his own son, and sent him to die so that we could each have the chance to live! This act sent the strong signal that God isn't holding *anything* back to help us. Everything's on the table!

Here's a prayer to help you take advantage of this S-O-S:

Dear God, I realize that there's nothing too hard for you. There's nothing impossible with you. I also know that there's no limit to your love for me and your desire to see me do well in life. I thank you for the comfort of your power and the assurance of your love for me. Let your power and love work on my behalf to bring about what's best for me in this situation. Thank you again for your unfailing, unending love for me. In Jesus' name I pray, amen.

S-O-S #8: Release the situation into God's care—and stop meddling.

Releasing the situation into God's care is one of the most liberating experiences you'll ever know. It's also one of the toughest to learn.

I have no problems releasing a situation in prayer (verbally); my struggle comes with actually letting things go *mentally* and *emotionally*. Sometimes I worry about the situation until I reclaim it, even though I had given it to God only minutes before.

Worrying, for many of us, is as natural as yawning when we're sleepy. We obsess, stress, and worry subconsciously. We can't seem to control these tortuous thought patterns.

The ancient Greeks used the word *merimna* to describe this kind of fixated thinking. *Merimna* denotes distractions, anxieties, burdens, and worries. The word comes from two separate Greek root words: *meiro* (to divide) and *noos* (the mind). *Merimna* identifies the real problem—a divided mind.

The scriptures call this "divided-mind" condition being "double-minded." Double-mindedness literally means to have two brains or two souls—both out of sync. Double-mindedness is a mugger's knife to fruitful living. Not only will it prevent us from making necessary decisions, it also hinders us from hearing God's voice clearly.

Here's a three-step method for dealing with double-mindedness.

First, we *recall* an occasion where God worked positively in our behalf. We turn our thoughts away from the current mental conflict and towards a personal testimony of a specific blessing.

Secondly, we *rejoice* over this testimony, re-living the experience. We enjoy the memory and give God praise, thanksgiving, and adoration for that victory.

Thirdly, we subconsciously *release* the stress and worry about our present situation as we delight ourselves in the joy of this blessed memory. We position ourselves to move forward by reminding ourselves of God's prior working in our lives.

Recall, rejoice, and *release.* Let me give you a personal example of this method in action.

When I was in my mid-twenties I noticed a growth on the left side of my chest. It started out very small, but within weeks it had grown to about the size of a quarter. It was very sensitive and painful to the touch. I had no idea what it was, but you can imagine the negative thoughts that came to mind. Was it cancer? Was it some kind of tumor? Ultimately I decided to deal with it in a way you're probably familiar with—I tried to ignore it. That *didn't* work.

Around this time I heard a sermon about praying to God for healing and not worrying once you had prayed. I'd heard similar messages before, but this time I was inspired.

Later that evening I prayed for healing and sensed a release of spiritually energy. I went to bed that night with great confidence, fully expecting to be completely healed the next morning. However, the next morning I was awakened by a sharp, familiar pain when I rolled over onto my chest.

With the sermon from the previous night fresh in my mind, instead of panicking I started thanking God for my healing. This worked as a diversion for a while, but shortly after I stopped my mini-praise session, I found my mind drifting back to worried thoughts about my situation. This pattern repeated itself throughout the day, and by day's end I was mentally exhausted and had a throbbing headache.

I repeated this same process over and over for the next week or so. On top of the painful knot in my chest, I was now stressing myself out. Relief finally came one evening when I came across a scripture that changed everything:

Rejoice in the Lord always. I will say it again: Rejoice!

Let your gentleness be evident to all. The Lord is near.

Do not be anxious about anything, but in everything, by prayer and petition, with thanksgiving, present your requests to God.

And the peace of God, which transcends all understanding, will guard your hearts and your minds in Christ Jesus.

Finally, brothers, whatever is true, whatever is noble, whatever is right, whatever is pure, whatever is lovely, whatever is admirable—if anything is excellent or praiseworthy—think about such things. (Phil. 4:4–8 NIV)

I noticed that the first verse says to "re"-joice. I knew that the prefix "re" means to do again, to go back and do over. It struck me that this passage wasn't talking about being joyful about something I hoped for in the future (like healing). Instead it was talking about reliving an experience from the past.

Verse 6 talks about presenting our requests to God with thanksgiving. Again, I noticed that the word used in this text for thanksgiving (Greek—*eucharista*) refers to a person who's focused on a *past* blessing. Verse 8 of this passage instructed me to meditate on *past* experiences that are praiseworthy.

As I lay there, it all began to come together like pieces of a puzzle. The key was in shifting the focus from present hardships to past (or even current) blessings.

The next morning I spent a few moments thanking God for healing the growth in my chest, but for the remainder of the day, whenever the thought of the growth came to mind, I would shift my focus to some past event in which God had shown his mercy and might on my behalf. I just praised God and thanked him for the things he had already done.

This kept me on an even emotional keel and also built a consciousness about God's faithfulness that had been missing up until then. The key was in praising God about *something* that literally had *nothing* to do with my current situation.

I don't actually know when the lump disappeared. I can't recall if it gradually shrunk or if it just vanished all at once. I do know that one day I realized it was gone. By the time it left, I had conquered the worry and learned how to truly release my problem to God.

One more word of advice: when you focus on experiences from your past, be sure to take the time to relive the experience.

For example, if God brought you through a difficult trial, think about the circumstances that led up to the trial. How did you get in that situation in the first place? Retrace the steps you took along the pathway of deliverance from the trial. Who did God bring into your life to help you through that time? Take a moment, give them a call, and tell them how much you appreciated them at the time.

Relive the feelings of joy you had when you realized that the trial was ending. Where were you when it was finally over? What scriptures helped you as you went through this challenge? Remember all of the tastes and sounds of the experience, and give yourself time to sit before the throne of God and talk with him about that experience. Laugh again. Cry again. Rejoice in God's presence again. Revelation 12:11 puts it like this: "And they overcame him by the blood of the Lamb and by the word of their testimony."

The word of your testimony—your account of the things God has done for you—is a mysterious weapon that God has equipped you with to help you overcome your trials, tests, and challenges.

Here's a prayer that'll help you initiate this key S-O-S:

Dear Lord, I thank you that I can come to you and cast all my cares on you today. Help me to remain at peace and to move forward with joy as I release this situation into your faithful hands. I rejoice in the many, many wonderful things

that you've already done for me. In addition, I choose to
rejoice instead of worry about this situation. Thank You
again, I love you. In Jesus' name, amen.

S-O-S #9: Pray that God's will be done in your situation.

It's a challenge to discuss the subject of the will of God without using some theological terminology (which, believe it or not, I've tried to avoid as much as possible). I'll try to keep this simple and brief, but there are some basic theological concepts that can't be avoided if any of this is really going to make sense.

To begin with, understand that everything that happens in life is due to an *act of will*. Any activity that builds up, tears down, or results in a change in this world can be directly attributed to an act of will. Will exists in different varieties. For example, there's human will, satanic or demonic will, and the Divine will. Additionally, God has designed the universe so magnificently that nature appears to have its own will and intelligence (technically, nature has a force, not a will).

The earth is the place where all these different "wills" have influence (see Ps. 8:3–6; Heb. 2:6–8). Human will, for example, has legitimate ability to change things happening on earth, but no bearing on what's taking place in the billions of other galaxies or in heaven. All will (including God's Divine will) operates within the structure of God's authority (which exists within the boundaries of God's supremacy).

Okay, let's step away from the seminary lecturn and get back to plain language. Think of the various forces of will as vehicles on the road. All of these "vehicles" are traveling on the same roads and they're all subject to the rules of the road—rules that have been defined and enforced by God's authority. God's authority acts like a traffic cop, allowing some acts of will to proceed, delaying other acts of will, and pulling some acts of will off the road altogether and towing them off to an impound yard.

God even subjects his own Divine will to this design and authority, so that even though he has all power, he doesn't automatically exercise that power in ways that violate the limitations and rules that he's put in place to keep creation in order. For example, it's clearly God's will for everyone to have a vibrant relationship with him—but he won't force anyone into such a relationship. God doesn't violate human free will, even though he has the power to do so.

So the question is, when different vehicles (wills) reach the same intersection all at once, what determines who gets the right of way? Here's the normal sequence of precedence of wills:

1. Forces of Nature—this includes all of the laws of physics and nature, like, for example, the sequence of the seasons, gravity, the earth's rotation; laws that govern human interaction with the environment, such as getting sick as a result of eating meat tainted with salmonella. The will of nature is fixed, sequential, and consequential.

2. Designated authority—this includes legal human will, including individual choice as well as governmental authority and God-ordained dominion over the resources of the planet.

3. Usurped authority—this includes unsanctioned use of influence by fallen spiritual beings or humans.

Notice that God's Divine will isn't included on the list. The reason for this is that God has established his Divine will to work in harmony and subjection to his revealed Word, initiated by the faith of a person who's operating within the structure of the authority God has established in that particular situation. Once a person invites God to intervene in a situation (by faith), then "God's will" begins to work in that situation. Otherwise, the Divine will sits idling on the side of the road like a car waiting to merge into traffic.

When we pray that God's will be done, God's Divine will comes on the scene like a fire engine barreling down the street with lights flashing and sirens blasting; all the other vehicles (wills) on the road have to pull off to the side or risk the consequence of being flattened as God's Divine will comes barreling through!

When we choose not to harmonize with God's plan (either as an act of ignorance, neglect or rebellion), then other forces are allowed to dominate that situation (temporarily). Even though the results are often disastrous, they're still allowed. However, they're also reversible. No matter how deep the roots, wrong is always wrong and it will never be a permanent condition in God's scheme of things.

God's Divine will doesn't always happen automatically, it has to be put in motion through the release of our faith in prayer or action. However, don't think that God's will can be excluded perpetually. God will eventually raise someone up who'll understand and pray for the entrance of his will—you can count on it. More importantly, you can make up your mind to be that someone.

Jesus taught his disciples to pray to the Father that his will be done and his kingdom rule would come to the earth just as it exists in heaven (see Lk. 11:2). It's important that we realize the significance of what Jesus is asking us to do.

God's Divine will isn't just going to happen automatically for you or me. It's our responsibility to understand his will for a situation and to set ourselves in agreement with his will through prayer.

As precious children of God, we have an inherited right to stand in agreement with our heavenly Father and pray that his will be done in our situation—regardless of what we actually see taking place. Even when we may not know what his specific will is in a given situation, by proclaiming, "Thy will be done," we set the wheels in motion for his intervention and his revelation of what his will is in that situation.

You can put this S-O-S in motion by simply praying the following:

Dear Heavenly Father, in this situation let your will be done.
In Jesus' name, amen.

S-O-S #10: WAIT.

"As for me, I look to the LORD for help. I *wait* [emphasis added] confidently for God to save me, and my God will certainly hear me"
(Mic. 7:7 NLT).

The final S-O-S on the list is probably the one you'll need to
spend the most time on. That's because this S-O-S contains the disciplines and exercises that you'll need to apply while you're waiting
for your circumstances to change or reach their conclusion.

If you've ever planted a garden or a seed, then you may have a
good idea of the importance of this S-O-S. Whenever you plant a
vegetable garden, for example, the first stage is to prepare the soil.
This usually includes tasks like clearing out the weeds, adding fer-
tilizer or other additives to the soil, and tilling the soil. Once this is
done, you plant the seeds into the ground and cover them.

The next stage is the most important for determining the size
and quality of your harvest: pre-growth care. This includes making
sure the garden is watered regularly, keeping out harmful rodents,
birds or other threats that would eat the seed, and making sure that
weeds or unwanted plants don't sprout up in the garden.

That's what this S-O-S addresses. It helps you understand
what you should be doing while waiting for your prayers to be
answered, your situation to change, or your harvest to come in. I
address this S-O-S with the word WAIT, an acronym, but also an
accurate description of what you'll be doing until your circumstances change or your trial reaches its conclusion. WAIT stands
for "*Worship-Anticipate-Irrigate-Trust.*"

Your actions during this waiting period will often determine whether your life moves forward with purpose or stumbles

repeatedly backwards like Sisyphus' boulder. Let's look at each of these disciplines individually.

Worship

The word "worship" is often used interchangeably with the word "praise," but there's a significant difference between the two. The final verse in the book of Psalms says, "Let everything that has breath *praise* the Lord."

Everything that has breath includes sinners as well as saints, birds as well as bees. Everything is all-inclusive, not distinguishing one breathing thing from another. Psalms 145:10 further states, "All thy works shall praise thee." This expands the list of who praises God from *things that breathe* to all creation. This would include oceans, trees, stars, and mountains.

The Hebrew word most often translated praise (*halal*) means to acknowledge a notable accomplishment. The mere existence of a hummingbird praises God. The fact that you can hold your hand up in front of your face and wiggle your fingers reflects praise back to God. The beautiful rainbow complimenting the snow-capped mountains and framed by the bluest sky all praise to God. The images throughout creation unconsciously stand as proof of God's notable accomplishments—and everything that exists testifies to God's achievements.

Worship, on the other hand, is only available to *people* who have an established relationship with God. Jesus said that worship has to be carried out as a decisive spiritual act (something a mountain definitely can't do) and as an outgrowth of personal response to one's revelation about God (see Jn. 4:23–24). Creation doesn't worship God; that privilege is reserved for people, specifically the children of faith.

Worship isn't just singing, lifting your hands, or praying. It's an *interactive experience* with God that's very individual, very personal, and very intimate. Worship isn't necessarily formal, but it is structured and deeply meaningful.

It's like a husband and wife in the privacy of their bedroom. Her make-up and his work suit have come off. Her hair has been let down. They communicate and express their love for each other very openly, very genuinely, and very tenderly. They've looked forward to being together again like this and they display their intimacy with emotional and physical expressions of love and affection. Worship is like this.

Worship is intimate interaction that focuses on *who* God is, not *what* he's accomplished. It's between just you and God—even if it takes place in a room with thousands of other people, it's still between you and him alone. However, it's not just you appreciating him; it also involves him appreciating you. He points out how special you are to him, how much he enjoys your smile, your unique sense of humor, and your gifts.

Every person has been created to worship God, but to engage in a deep, meaningful worship experience doesn't come naturally to any of us. Here's a list of a few practices that will help you develop your worship life and enrich your worship experience:

- Are you a morning person, a midday person, or a night person? Determine what time of the day you're at your peak and schedule at least thirty minutes of your peak time to spend alone with God.
- Make music a part of your worship time with the Lord. Music bypasses our stresses and helps set the right mood for what follows (i.e., whenever I come home and my wife has a hot bubble bath going, aromatic candles burning in the room, and Ramsey Lewis' *Hearts of Longing* playing softly, somehow I know we're not getting ready to do yard

work). Choose music or songs that help you relax and focus on who God really is. Put together a "mix CD" of different music tracks that you can play during your intimate times with God.

- Schedule a "date" with God. Pick at least one day during the week when you can schedule at least one hour of uninterrupted time with him. During this time, you can read the Bible or other books of faith that lift your spirit and draw your attention to him. Try to spend this hour in a quiet place where you're not likely to be interrupted. I like to take long walks through the woods on my "date" with God. Turn off your cell phone. You can pray or sing. You can just sit and listen to him. It's important to put it on the calendar and not allow it to be bumped around by other things that invariably pop up during the week.

- Get a notebook or a notepad and start a *meditation journal.* Keep track of Bible passages you read and any ideas that come to your spirit or your mind from God. Review the journal at least once a week; it'll become a map that shows were God has brought you from and where he's taking you.

Anticipate

I love the Encarta Dictionary's definition of the word "anticipate": *expect something!*[8] Anticipate means to expect, to look forward to something—something specific! To be fairly certain that *something specific* is going to happen.

I'm not talking about some kind of anxious, breathless eagerness that borders on obsession, but rather a confident expectation that God is going to perform exactly what he said he would perform. The key to this kind of anticipation is focusing on the finished, finished, finished *work of Jesus Christ.* We've been given an entire set of spiritual rights and privileges that are to be enacted *in this life*—all because of what Jesus Christ has already accomplished for us!

Let me give an example from American history. In 1920 the Nineteenth Amendment was added to the US Constitution. This gave women the right to vote on the same terms as men, culminating a suffrage movement that had lasted over 125 years. Today, any female citizen of legal age can take advantage of the privilege to vote in any local, state, or federal election. She doesn't have to file a lawsuit or organize a protest march in order to be allowed to vote—those battles have already been fought and decided. They're over . . . *finished*!

In the same sense, Jesus has provided rights and privileges for each of us through his *finished* work, but it's up to us to know what they are and how to enact them—otherwise it's as if they don't even exist.

A good place to start is to simply read the New Testament and make a list of all the passages that contain phrases such as "in Christ," "through Christ," "in Him," or "through Him." Keep your eyes open for any passages that describe the benefits we have as believers. These are literally our spiritual Bill of Rights. Here are a few examples:

> . . . you are complete *in Him* [emphasis added], who is the head of all principality and power (Col. 2:10).

> But God has given you a place *in Christ Jesus* [emphasis added], through whom God has given us wisdom and righteousness and salvation, and made us holy (1 Cor. 1:30).

> I can do all things *through Christ* [emphasis added] who strengthens me (Phil 4:13).

> Yet in all these things we are more than conquerors *through Him* [emphasis added] who loved us (Rom. 8:37).

Remember that God is the God who *rewards those who believe*—those who expect him to come through on what he has said. This isn't based on some qualifying act we're expected to perform, but on the liberating work of Jesus Christ, a completed work that endows each of us with specific rights and privileges.

Anticipation in this regard means to set our affections and attention on the things that God has promised, to have a settled hope based on what God has said in his word . . . and to look for that hope to materialize.

Insert your name in the scriptures and understand that the promises of God are meant for you—personally! Meditate on the things that God has already done for you in the past, and dwell on his faithfulness as a promissory for the things you expect him to work out for you in the future.

Irrigate

To irrigate means to water, to counteract dryness with moisture. While you're waiting on your situation to change, there are two areas you need to make sure get plenty of "water" so they don't dry out.

The first is *people* around you. When Jesus hung on the cross, during his most trying moments of life, he stopped to see to the needs of those closest to him. He comforted his mother by asking his friend John to see to it that she was provided for. He reached out to the dying thief on the cross next to him and assured him that his suffering would soon be replaced with rest in paradise.

It's important to do what you can to encourage or help those that are close to you. Close in terms of relationship (family and relatives) as well as in terms of proximity (your neighbor across the street or the person who works in the next cubicle).

The second area you need to make sure to water is *yourself*. Don't let your spirit or your soul dry out. Don't let your body wear down.

Water yourself by reading God's Word daily, but also by fellowshipping with other believers regularly, laughing out loud often, getting some physical exercise, eating foods that give you energy, spending quiet moments in prayer, and revisiting pleasant places and experiences from your past. Don't lose sight of who you are in the midst of what you're going through. Keep yourself spiritually hydrated.

Trust

On one occasion, the Bible describes a conversation between Jesus and Peter prior to Peter becoming a follower of Jesus. Peter was a professional fisherman who, along with several of his co-workers, had just finished his regular shift on the fishing boat. After fishing all night, they hadn't caught a single fish. Jesus told Peter that if he would cast his net into the deepest part of the lake his fortunes would change. Here's Peter's response: "Master, we toiled all night [exhaustingly] and caught nothing [in our nets]. But on the ground of Your word, I will lower the nets [again]" (Lk. 5:5 AMP).

Peter's reply revealed a reluctant skepticism that most of us can identify with. A popular cliché says, "Insanity is doing the same thing over and over and expecting different results." It seems as if Jesus was asking Peter to do the same thing that he had been doing—a task that Peter was all too familiar with and whose outcome could be predicted.

However, Jesus wasn't asking Peter to do the same thing. Peter's earlier fishing experience was all based on his resources. However, the second time out he took something different with him onto the lake—the command and promise of God. As a result, they caught so many fish that their nets began to rip apart and the boat began to sink under the weight of such a remarkable haul!

God's Word will not return unfulfilled. Still, it requires someone who's motivated by trust to activate it. Trust is simply taking God at his word. Even in the routine events of life that seem predictable, boring, and unrelenting—trust God.

I love the following quote from Hannah Whitehall Smith, which puts the issue of trusting God in context:

> *You find no difficulty in trusting the Lord with the management of the universe, and all the outward creation, and can your case be any more complex or difficult than these, that you need to be anxious or troubled about his management of you? Away with such unworthy doubting! Take your stand on the power and trustworthiness of your God, and see how quickly all difficulties will vanish before a steadfast determination to believe. Trust in the dark, trust in the light, trust at night and trust in the morning, and you will find that the faith which may begin by mighty effort, will end sooner or later by becoming the easy and natural habit of the soul.*[9]

The bottom line is that God is worth trusting . . . or trustworthy!

Epilogue

I pray and hope that you've grown from what you've read in the last two chapters. It's important to remember that the anchor encourages you to Space *Yourself*—not your spouse, your child, a relative, friend, or associate. Make sure that *you're* learning, growing, and implementing these principles in *your own* life.

God wants you to learn to properly manage everything he's given you—including what appears to be empty space. *Spacing Yourself* teaches you to work within God's framework for life, dealing with every pleasant and unpleasant experience effectively so he can accomplish what he wants in you by working through your circumstances.

He wants you to learn to trust him to fill in (as well as work in) all the "spaces" of your life—especially the seemingly empty spaces. I think that one of the best things we can offer God is a blank slate, because it gives him an opportunity to fill it with whatever is needed. He's at his absolute best when he's working with the absolute least. All he's asking from you . . . is a little space.

Space Yourself.

Chapter 4

PACE
YOURSELF

God's timing, seasons, and you

Time goes you say? Ah no! Alas, Time stays, we go![10]
—THE PARADOX OF TIME

Life is full of paradoxes. For example, we are finite creatures living in an infinite cosmos. Our existence is framed by borders
within an unframed, borderless continuum.

Time is one of the administrators of this unframed, borderless
continuum. Time patiently presents the universe to us in sixty-sec-
ond increments, each moment powerful enough to alter the rest of
our lives. Time employs its own staff, and one of its most reliable
supervisors is the deadline.

Deadlines can be found everywhere you look in society. The
homework assignment, the spring clothing line, the income tax
return, the wedding gown—all of these have to be completed by specific deadlines. Entire businesses (i.e., UPS, FedEx) have been built
on their ability to meet deadlines.

In most cases, failure to meet a deadline results in an unpleasant consequence. That's why deadlines are excellent incentives when we find ourselves unorganized, distracted, unmotivated, or just plain lazy. Like the dichotomous forces of yin and yang, deadlines use the potential of negative consequences to produce positive movement in our lives.

Sitting atop the hill of all deadlines is death. It's the final deadline. There are many views about what happens on the other side of life's curtain, but most of us agree that our afterlife experience will begin with an unannounced blind date—with death.

This "ultimate deadline" doesn't end our existence, but it does end our activities here on earth. As Walter Scott put it so scenically,

Like the dew on the mountain,
Like the foam on the river,
Like the bubble on the fountain,
Thou art gone, and forever![11]

Many people live long, full lives before they die, but just as many seem to die much too soon. Whether the victims of sickness, tragedy, or some other unexpected event, the cemetery is filled with markers bearing the chiseled names of people who've come to life's ending before they had really finished living.

Many of them never achieved all the positive things that were within reach during their lifetime. Like a mismanaged budget, their lives ran out with something still owed, something left undone, something yet to be given.

Myles Munroe observed: "The cemetery represents the greatest single warehouse for life-changing ideas. Ideas which remain deathly silent—unexpressed and buried with the people who never succeeded in breathing life into their dreams."

Stop for just a moment, take a deep breath, and hold it for about five seconds. Now, let it out slowly and evenly, allowing yourself to feel your muscles relax as the escaping air releases stress throughout your body.

However soothing that breathing exercise may have been, it's easy to lose sight of the fact that each breath comes from a diminishing, non-replenishable inventory. Each breath takes us one step closer to our *final* breath; and when it comes to life's mysteries, there's no greater mystery than how such an unavoidable event as our "last breath" can remain such a well-kept secret. We know we'll draw our last breath one day, we just don't know *which* day.

The main question this chapter aims to address is this: "Is it possible to live in such a way—to pace myself—so that whenever death comes knocking (whether I'm nine or ninety) I can confidently say, 'I've finished what was meant for my life, I'm ready to go . . . I'm done.'?" It's quite a challenging question, but one that each of us must settle to help protect us from one of the deadliest threats to our faith.

When Faith Meets Time

After nearly dying from a prolonged illness, King David wrote the following words: "Show me, O LORD, my life's end and the number of my days; let me know how fleeting is my life" (Ps. 39:4).

He brings up a question most of us have thought about; "What if I knew the precise time and date of my death beforehand?"

If you had this information, how much in your life would really change? How much more value would each second have if you knew the exact number of seconds left in your account? What would it mean to you to know that you had exactly forty years . . . or five years . . . or only a few weeks left to live? What would you do differently regarding your relationships . . . your health . . . your career choices . . . your routine activities? What would "normal" look like for you then? If any of us could get our hands on this kind of information we'd certainly use it to our advantage. Or would we?

It might come as a surprise to know that the Bible calls an obsessive focus on this kind of knowledge "wicked" (see Matt. 16:4, Lk. 11:29). On more than one occasion, Jesus responded to people who were too caught up with end-time matters. He rebuked them, pointing out that not only is this type of attention improvident but actually evil.

The term "evil" basically means something that contends with God's will. So why does the Bible consider us having foreknowledge of the date we'll die as "something that contends with God's will?" Let's look at a few of the reasons.

First, we're naturally inclined to put off certain things until the last possible moment. When structure and discipline are absent, human nature tends to run like a wandering vine, twisting in and out of the lattices of its own self-serving interests. Even if we knew, for example, that we had exactly twenty years left to live, the majority of us would probably spend most of that time chasing our own interests. We'd wait until we had a few months left before we'd really get serious about developing a sincere relationship with God. Even then, our motives would lean towards making sure we're prepared for life after death—not in making ourselves available for meaningful service to God.

Secondly, imagine if you were abandoned in the thickest, deepest jungle in Jakarta. You have no idea where you are; you just know you desperately want to get out. Suddenly, you look up and see a parachute floating down from the sky with a small wooden box attached. When it lands, you open the box, and your heart leaps with hope as you view the two items inside: a detailed split-leather calendar/journal, and a top-of-the-line Swiss military field watch.

You soon realize, however, that your hope is misplaced; these items won't do anything to actually help you get out of the jungle.

When you're lost in the woods, you need a map or a compass—*not* a calendar or clock. To get through the forests of our own lives we need something to guide us, *not* something to simply keep track of time.

Faith is a *compass* mechanism. It helps guide us. On the other hand, knowing the date of our death is calendar and clock information. It's the kind of knowledge that dupes us into thinking it's more useful than it really is. It's also the type of knowledge that can actually work against the fundamental process of faith.

The process of faith calls on us to pursue our visions and dreams on a road that's sometimes so heavily draped in fog there's little visibility of what lies ahead. But even with such limited vision, we can still move forward confidently, seeing what can only be perceived by faith. The factor of "the unknown" about our lives is a key element of walking by faith. When mixed with hope, it creates a "spiritual tautness" that helps us move forward in life.

Pressing vs. Pressuring

What exactly is spiritual tautness? Spiritual tautness is a key factor for advancing through life by faith. Think of spiritual tautness in mountain-climbing terms. Climbers use a special rope attached to a harness to aid them during ascent or descent. They have to make sure that just the right amount of tautness is always present in the rope. If the rope is too tight then it restricts movement, making the climb nearly impossible. If too much slack is allowed then the rope could loosen and detach from its anchor, which could result in injury or worse for the climber.

Not knowing the date of our deaths is the kind of hidden knowledge that actually helps us maintain the right amount of spiritual tautness as we reach, by faith, for the heights in life.

The Bible gives spiritual tautness another name: *pressing*. For example, the passage that encourages us to "press towards the mark for the prize of the high calling" (see Phil. 3:14) actually refers to spiritual tautness. But understand the differences between *pressing* and *pressure*, between *tautness* and *tension*. The one force aids us in moving forward in life, while the other actually retards our efforts to advance.

Pressing works to build up our faith as we move forward in life. It causes us to develop the disciplines of focusing on God's promises, praying consistently, and relying on God's guidance in the face of strong resistance.

Pressure has the exact opposite effect. It comes to discourage our faith, cause us to abandon hope in God, and paralyze our movement.

Pressing is the force we exert against our circumstances. Pressure is the force our circumstances exert against us.

Pressure at the core is the spiritual threat I call the *"Running When You Should Be Walking and Walking When You Should Be Running"* Fury. This Fury plants a sophisticated seed of worry, anxiety, and uncertainty in our souls, specifically, worry attached to the concern that our activities aren't corresponding to what God really wants for us. As the harmful seed grows, we feel that we've missed God's will for our lives altogether, in some cases convinced that our past disobedience, ignorance, apathy, or procrastination has caused us to forfeit certain things meant for our good.

We lease mental space to the fear that we'll never experience what we've been created to do. The *Running When You Should Be Walking and Walking When You Should Be Running* Fury releases anxiety into our lives. These anxieties loiter in the dark corners of our souls, waiting for the opportunity to mug any passing thoughts of hope. They pull us towards darkness inch by inch, and puncture our souls so that the light of truth won't leak out.

When this Fury becomes established in our lives, it plants a nagging feeling that no matter what we're doing, there's something more fitting that we *should* be doing. It causes us to see our accomplishments as millstones rather than milestones. Finally, it destabilizes our faith by using anything unfulfilled from our past as an argument against our potential and our future.

The Races We Run

How does the *Running When You Should Be Walking and Walking When You Should Be Running* Fury actually become part of our lives? The most common way is through comparison *within* the faith community.

In one sense, life is like a race. In fact, the Bible makes multiple references to life as a race. However, when most people think of a race, they think of a competitive event, and it's easy to get off track when we apply the wrong elements of competition to our spiritual race.

The object of most races is to reach the finish line ahead of everyone else. During the race we'll find ourselves in one of three positions: out front leading the pack, somewhere in the middle of the pack, or lagging behind the pack.

If someone's ahead of us, we view ourselves in an *inferior* position to them. We put more pressure on ourselves and exert more energy to catch up. If someone's behind us, we view ourselves in a *superior* position. We're motivated to maintain our position, so we use our precious energy to make sure that we stay ahead of them. In either case, we're *pressuring inward* to perform against someone else—not *pressing onward* to gain the prize promised in God's Word.

These concepts of "superiority" and "inferiority" have no place in the life of faith, because they bind our sense of fulfillment with our relation to other people. They also generate negative internal pressuring that's the opposite of beneficial spiritual pressing.

If someone else has a larger ministry, a more God-fearing family, a more positive spiritual countenance, a broader spiritual vocabulary, or a more impressive spiritual pedigree, then we feel compelled (pressured) to match or exceed what they *appear* to be doing better than us. It's the spiritual version of keeping up with the Joneses, a dangerous covetousness coated with the veneer of spiritual aspiration.

But let's dig a little deeper. Sometimes we're not trying to keep up with other people around us. In fact, we may be so absorbed with our own lives that we're not even aware of what's going on with people around us. Even in many of those cases, we're often still driven by comparison. Not with people around us—but with those we hold up as heroes of the faith. We look at the achievements of people from the scriptures (like Moses, Esther, or Jonah), or notable men and women of faith of our times (like Billy Graham, Joyce Meyer, or Charles Mason), and use their achievements as a measuring stick for our own lives.

In either case, the result is that the pace for our spiritual lives isn't being "set by things above" but by things—or more accurately by people—below. These roads lead to the slippery banks of pressure, where many of our rising dreams slip into the raging waters of wasteful comparison.

In addressing the faith community of his day, the apostle Paul warned about falling into this same deceptive web: "But in measuring themselves by themselves and comparing themselves to themselves, they lack understanding" (2 Cor. 10:12 HCSB). When the pace of our lives is set by the achievements of other people, we're demonstrating our lack of understanding of the spiritual race. We also leave the door cracked so that the Running When You Should Be Walking and Walking When You Should Be Running Fury can gain entrance into our lives.

Our spiritual race isn't a competitive event against other people. But we're so used to setting and measuring goals against what others are doing that we may not even know another way to gauge what we're about. This brings us back to the question, "How do I pace myself so that whether I die at nine or at ninety, I can confidently say, "I've finished my race . . . I'm really done!"'"

Vision and Pace

Many people within the faith community insist that their pace should be determined by whatever vision God has given them. They believe that's the key to using their gifts for God's highest glory. This sounds sensible; the only problem is that the scriptures don't quite support it.

Take, for example, the Old Testament prophet Elijah. God gives Elijah specific instructions to anoint Hazael as king over Syria, to anoint Jehu as king over Israel, and to anoint Elisha to stand in the prophetic office as his replacement (see 1 Kgs. 19:15–16). You won't find a clearer vision and set of instructions in the Bible.

After receiving these instructions from God, Elijah anointed Elisha as his replacement but never got around to anointing the other two future kings—even though he lived at least an additional four years *after* he received these instructions! This incident is even more interesting in view of the fact that Elijah was one of the few people in the Bible to whom God actually told the exact date that he'd leave this earth (see 2 Kgs. 2).

If fulfilling his vision from God was that critical, it seems that he would have made sure that all of those tasks were completed before his time on earth was done. But even in the face of knowing exactly how much time he had left, the scriptures show no evidence of Elijah making any extra effort to fulfill the vision he'd been given four years earlier. In spite of this apparent failure, Elijah was still welcomed into paradise—escorted by a glorious chariot of fire, the likes of which has never been repeated.

Elijah doesn't stand alone on the list of champions of the faith who walked devotedly before God yet failed to accomplish all of the things that God's vision for their lives had set forth. In fact, Hebrews 11—often referred to as the "Hall of Faith"—points out a number of great men and women of God who never actually reached the faith milestones for which they were aiming.

From this it's clear that vision gives us a sense of spiritual focus, but it's not meant to actually set the pace for our lives. So the question remains: how do I actually pace myself?

Pace Yourself 101

Pace Yourself is the second anchor in this book, and it provides the key to overcoming the Running When You Should Be Walking and Walking When You Should Be Running Fury. When the pace of our lives is fully synchronized with God, it eliminates the deceptive claims suggested by this Fury.

A solid pace (or pulse) is one of the clearest indicators of good health. Medical studies show that three primary factors determine a healthy pace. They are:

1. Rhythm—the regularity of the pulse beats and the intervals between each beat
2. Volume—the strength or force of the pulse
3. Rate—the actual number of beats per minute

Similarly, when it comes to our spiritual lives, three primary factors determine a healthy spiritual pace. They are:

1. Rhythm—something that meets God's purpose working through us daily
2. Volume—something that reflects the intensity of God's glory working in us
3. Rate—something that can be accomplished over a lifetime—as well as in the very next moment

I've discovered something that satisfies all three requirements. It can be found in Jesus' own words: "Just as the Son of Man came not to be waited on but to *serve*, and to *give his life* as a *ransom for many* [the price paid to set them free]" (Matt. 20:28 AMP).

Serving is the key to setting the proper pace for one's life; or more specifically, *serving heaven's way*. Serving heaven's way is unique. It glorifies our creator, flowing from the storage of goodness God has built into each of our spirits.

The scriptures speak of servanthood as a highly esteemed value among God's people. Paul dismissed the hardships of his life's mission by reminding us that he considered himself God's slave or bondman. I'd like to suggest a term that draws from these concepts to represent the kind of life the Pace Yourself anchor truly calls for: *bondhood*.

Bondhood is heaven's gold standard for serving, and fully embodies the anchor to *Pace Yourself*. It also meets all three requirements for setting the proper pace for our spiritual lives.

1. Bondhood reflects God's glory working in us.
2. Bondhood utilizes our unique gifts to meet God's purpose working through us.
3. Bondhood can be accomplished over a lifetime—as well as in the very next moment.

Bondhood, or Pacing Yourself, isn't just a lot of religious movement and effort. It's not just a checklist of good deeds. This type of serving is a powerful expression of faith that flows out of an attitude that's been cultivated, purged, and tried within the framework of a wholesome mind.

It doesn't come to us naturally, but can be learned and developed over time, following the sequence taught in 1 Corinthians 13:11. This passage explains that spiritual things ripen as we first learn to discipline how we think (thought as a child), which positions us to display the right attitude (understood as a child), which, in turn, helps us to disciple our tongue (spoke as a child).

Pacing Yourself isn't a place we come to as a matter of luck, fate, or spiritual destiny. It's an anchor that we latch on to deliberately.

Jesus was the perfect example of this type of service. The scripture points out that Jesus had to learn active, special obedience through difficult life experiences (see Heb. 5:8 AMP). He understood that his time on earth—his life—was a unique asset given to him by the Father. He realized that the highest return on his life would result from investing in the lives of others *through service.*

He viewed every encounter with others as an opportunity to invest something . . . to leave something behind . . . to add something to their lives that would help them experience a better life. From the lowly beggar to the high-ranking official—when it came to interacting with other people, Jesus focused on serving heaven's way.

As God's children, we must each learn the same lessons. Pacing Yourself isn't a behavior that happens automatically or just because we're part of the faith community. We're required to make an investment in understanding and applying this key spiritual anchor.

What's Culture Got to Do with It?

Bondhood is a reflection of heaven's culture. Culture is an institutionalized set of attitudes, values, and practices that characterizes a specific group. For example, the Hupda tribe of the Amazon rainforest has a distinct culture that includes living in wall-less huts, hunting peccaries for food, and regularly using psychoactive plants like Patu and Carpi to help them make choices regarding tribal affairs. That's very different from the culture of people who live in Milford, Connecticut.

Culture isn't bound to geographical borders or specific environments—culture is moveable. We carry culture with us wherever we go. Furthermore, we can study other cultures and integrate useful features from them into our own.

The more cultures we're exposed to and learn from, the bigger our lives become. Cultural thinking is a way we reconcile the attitudes, values, and practices of a different culture to our own.

Cultural thinking expands life dramatically. It's what Jesus was talking about when he looked out on a teeming multitude and said, "Take my yoke upon you and *learn of me*" [italics added] (see Matt. 11:28). This was an invitation for the crowd to expand their lives through understanding heaven's culture—the most alien culture to man.

The majority of Jesus' teaching and preaching focused on the Kingdom of Heaven—and the *culture of heaven.* People of his day had a hard time understanding his teachings and ministry because they presumed his miraculous works came from secret formulas and magical powers—secrets that could only be accessed by a chosen few.

Many people in today's faith community have these same ideas. However, it's clear that Christ's healings, miracles, and other works of power had nothing to do with magic or mystical secrets. They had everything to do with understanding heaven's culture.

Multi-cultural expression is fairly common in the United States, my home country. While it is encouraged here, our government still regulates these cultural expressions. For example, in some cultures a man can marry several wives at once, but that's not allowed in the United States. Within its borders, the U.S. government determines what can and cannot be allowed—it reigns supreme over any other cultural expressions.

However, when it comes to the Kingdom of Heaven, the policies of the United States government go right out the window. It's impossible to separate the culture of heaven from the government (or authority) of heaven. The culture of heaven exists and is maintained by the authority of the Word of God, which is the expression of the will of God.

The authority of God's Word *is* the government of heaven, and no earthly government or authority can put any restriction on what God has spoken. So, whenever there's a display of the culture of heaven here on the earth, not only does it override any other culture, but also the government of heaven is brought to bear in the situation to enforce it—even if it means overruling other governments or authorities.

Wherever there is an expression of heaven's culture in the earth (i.e. a person is healed from a disease, delivered from a destructive habit, cured from emotional trauma, born into the family of God, etc.), what actually takes place is the authority of the Kingdom of Heaven overrules any other authority, and the supernatural order of heaven's culture overrides the natural order of things here on earth.

Bondhood releases the influence of heaven's culture into the earth. It's one of the ways that the third segment of the Lord's Prayer is fulfilled: "Thy kingdom come, thy will be done on earth as it is in heaven" (Matt. 6:9–13). It's a heaven-facing approach to carrying out the duties and responsibilities of serving—based strictly on heaven's definition of service.

Let's look at heaven's description of service in detail:

Think of yourselves the way Christ Jesus thought of himself. He had equal status with God but didn't think so much of himself that he had to cling to the advantages of that status no matter what. Not at all. When the time came, he set aside the privileges of deity and took on the status of a *slave*, became human! Having become human, he stayed human. It was an incredibly humbling process. He didn't claim special privileges. Instead, he lived a *selfless, obedient* life and then died a *selfless, obedient* death [emphasis added]. (Phil. 2:5–8 AMP)

The word "slave" in this passage comes from the Greek word *doulos*, which means "devoted to another to the disregard of one's own interests."[12] Although many Bible translations use the softer term "servant," the word "slave" is much more accurate. According to the *Theological Dictionary of the New Testament*, the term refers to "service which is not a matter of choice for the one who renders it, which he has to perform whether he likes or not, because he is subject as a slave to an alien will, to the will of his owner."[13]

Not only does the word denote the surrender of one's will, but it also denotes ownership by another, which means completely surrendering one's freedom.

There's no wiggle room in the type of service that God requires and honors. It can be described as a unique, transformational form of voluntary slavery. We, as God's children (and of our own accord), forfeit our freedoms, rights, and privileges for the opportunity to become members of his elite group of heart-crafted slaves. Moreover, even though we're part of his family, most common rules of slavery still apply.

We're required to do exactly as he expects of us without questioning his wisdom. Our feelings about what we're asked to do are set aside. You've heard of blind faith? Pacing Yourself *is* blind obedience. The concepts of fairness don't come into play when it comes to this kind of service. We're no longer free to do as we please, to come and go as we please, or to choose the task that seems most suitable for our abilities.

Like most slaves, we aren't paid for the services we render (at least not in this life—I'll clarify this later in the chapter). Our service is given for the pleasure of God our master, and most often for the benefit of others. This is what it means to serve heaven's way, and this is the type of serving that, when carried out on the earth, sets the proper pace for one's life.

Pace Yourself 201

Each day provides multiple opportunities for us to serve. Some opportunities are obvious, others are disguised. Regardless, each opportunity to serve is a transformational event, affecting us as well as those who benefit from our service.

Here are a few key points to remember about the goals of bondhood:

1. Bondhood allows God to extend his touch of love to others through us.
2. Bondhood is carried out for the benefit of other people (whether they're present or absent, aware or unaware of your actions).
3. Bondhood releases the winds of transformation into the atmosphere.
4. Bondhood pleases God and gives him joy.
5. Bondhood precedes change; it paves the way for unforeseen miracles.
6. Bondhood isn't performed for personal acknowledgement, appreciation, or notice (at least not from other people).
7. Bondhood supports the Holy Spirit's ongoing work of sanctification in us and others.

Regarding point #7, we should remember that no matter how successful people around us seem to be, there are still areas in their lives that are undeveloped or even bound. Everyone has issues that resist growth, mending, or wholeness in their souls.

This was driven home during the years I lived in Palm Springs, California. It's called the getaway to the stars, and the population included celebrities from all walks of life: movie stars, corporate leaders, even retired presidents. We were fortunate to become acquainted with many of these celebrities through both ministry and business.

Their wealth, status, and accomplishments afforded them a privileged and carefree life—at least from an outsider's view. But an insider's view showed that these accomplished people faced incredible complications in their lives (in addition to the same common challenges most of us deal with).

God uses bondhood as a way for us to help others continue to grow and move forward in their lives. In many cases, bondhood helps to free others from the bondages of sin or its collateral damages in their life. Each act of *serving* can literally *sever* a link from the chain that holds an individual in some form of bondage. For every life-restricting chain we remove off someone else's life through bondhood, we'll experience a corresponding increase of liberty in our own lives.

Pace in Practical Terms

Almost every encounter with other people brings with it a practical opportunity for us to serve in some way. When we were expecting our first child, we enrolled in a Lamaze class. Our friends Joe and Teri, who at the time were assistant pastors at the church we were attending, also enrolled in the same class.

There were about ten couples in the class. The instructor was sensitive to the fact that these pregnant women had a lot of extra pressure on their bladders, so we had plenty of breaks throughout the class. During the breaks, many of us would make a beeline for the refreshment table. There were cookies, pastries, and two beverage dispensers—one with water and one with punch. I noticed that during our breaks, Joe would stand next to the beverage dispenser and serve water or punch to people as they came over to the table.

This struck me as being a little odd because, for one thing, Joe was a pastor. In the circles that I grew up in, pastors were usually given preferential treatment (especially when it came to free food). But Joe served these people in a very practical way—and although it wasn't his goal, his actions stuck out and were noticed by others in the class as well. It was a demonstration of bondhood.

The degree of success or failure, victory or defeat, progress or stagnation that we'll experience in many of life's situations can often be traced directly to what we think about in that situation. Notice, I didn't say *how* we think about the situation, but *what* we think about in it. This is especially true when it comes to bondhood.

How we think is a broad, generic outlook that puts us in the right neighborhood. *What* we think puts us on the actual doorstep of the right home *in* that neighborhood.

What you think takes the broader view of how you think and gives it focused, practical expression in your specific situation. We can accept the basic idea that we should serve others (how we think), but until we come up with some specific action of service (what we think) then all of our thoughts are nothing more than daydreaming exercises.

Be very specific in your thinking about ways to serve those around you, especially in the routine situations of your life. For example, you can serve in your home by helping others with their chores or by surprising them and doing some of their chores for them. In the grocery store we can help people load their groceries in their car. We could offer to help a co-worker who's running behind on a project. My neighbor, who's in his seventies, will often come over and mow my front lawn whenever he mows his front lawn.

Look around you and quietly observe the needs of the people near you. Then, being sensitive to the leading of God's Spirit, make a decision to serve those people by meeting some of their needs.

You can also serve those around you through consistent prayer. For example, I love the outdoors and each morning I try to walk, jog, or ride my bike through the nature trails near my home. I also use this time to pray specifically for my neighbors. I cover our community with prayers for everything that makes up a strong community: interceding for marriages, safety, friendships, health, careers, employment, education, etc.

Pace Yourself 301

Bondhood produces good energy—in us and around us. In spite of that fact, it isn't always an easy road. Sometimes simple and sincere acts of service are met with ridicule, criticism, and other similar attacks. Sadly, sometimes the resistance and resentment can even reach the life-threatening level.

Dr. Martin Luther King Jr. often acknowledged this as he pursued his lifelong commitment to improve mankind's condition through bondhood. The occasion of his last public appearance was a labor dispute involving sanitation workers in Memphis, Tennessee. In a speech on their behalf, he mentioned the ongoing threats he had received on his life because of his commitment to service. He didn't dismiss the threats, but he said his ultimate decision came down to this: "People have asked me if I'm worried about if I help the sanitation workers, what will happen to me? But for me, the real question is, 'If I do not try to help the sanitation worker, what will happen to them?'"

When faced with the choice of standing on the sidelines while these workers struggled, or trying to make a difference through serving heaven's way, Dr. King chose the path of bondhood. His choice reminds me of the quote often attributed to Edmund Burke, "The only thing necessary for the triumph of evil is for good men to do nothing." In both cases, there's a clear understanding that bondhood is a means of confronting and thwarting the evil that exists in society.

Pacing Yourself through bondhood confronts social and spiritual malformations and creates a path for God's divine power to flow into our world and change someone's life for the better.

Still, even when I choose to serve heaven's way, there's no guarantee that I can actually follow through with my choice. I've personally failed to follow through with my lofty prayer-closet decisions to serve more times than I care to think about. Inner resistance will be one of our biggest obstacles when we decide to serve heaven's way. Either we won't *feel* like serving (emotional resistance) or we just won't *want* to serve (resistance of the will). Here are some keys to overcoming these two challenges.

Servant's Key #1

The first key is to eliminate the element of choice. In the second chapter of the Gospel of John, we read about the first miracle that Jesus ever performed—turning water into vintage wine. Jesus' mother became involved with events leading up to this miracle. Let's look at what she told some of the attendants at the wedding: "His mother said to the servants, *'Do whatever he tells you'*" [italics added] (Jn. 2:5 NLT).

Simple—but to the point. "Just do what he says." Doing what Jesus says isn't always easy, but it is always doable! Sometimes we'll need to put the soundtrack of our minds on "mute" and just obey God.

Remember, bondhood requires us to submit ourselves to slavery—literally. With this in mind, we must approach the opportunity to serve with an intense determination to do whatever God tells us to do. Regardless of how we feel about it . . . regardless of our history with that person or in similar circumstances . . . regardless of how embarrassing or stupid it will look.

Don't think about it.

Don't analyze it.

Don't question it.

Simply obey and do it.

We'll each need to develop a disciplined surrender to God. Meditate on exactly what you're going to do in a given situation, and when the opportunity arises, do it. It may not "feel" right, but don't let that distract you. Our feelings are usually the last part of our nature to accept anything new from God. Remember, if we can crucify out internal conflicts, God can be glorified in our pace.

Servant's Key #2

The second key follows the first. It's simply this: learn how to draw on the strength that's available to us from heaven in order to fulfill our commitment to bondhood. No one in human form can serve heaven's way without direct assistance from heaven.

Even Jesus had to pray for help to suppress his human will and desires, which stood in resistance to his upcoming trial of the cross. If Jesus needed to get help in order to complete his commitment to serve, it should come as no surprise that you and I have to travel down the same road.

Many times we won't have the willpower or the energy to carry out some of these difficult acts of service. Don't panic—God knew this would be the case all along. That's when we have to look for help that can only come from an external source. How do we do this? Primarily through prayer—*followed by decisive action.*

Meditation on God's changeless promises combined with fixing our sights on the end results will also help us fulfill our commitment to bondhood. Take a look at how the book of Hebrews addresses the issue:

> Looking away [from all that will distract] to Jesus, Who
> is the Leader and the Source of our faith [giving the first

incentive for our belief] and is also its Finisher [bringing
it to maturity and perfection]. He, for the joy [of obtaining
the prize] that was set before Him, *endured the cross,
despising and ignoring the shame* [italics added], and is
now seated at the right hand of the throne of God. (Heb
12:2–3 AMP)

Learn to meditate on the finish line ... the projected outcome ... the
expected and desired end result. That's the real prize. Don't let emotional conflicts or willful resistance distract you from what needs to
be done. If you want to move forward in your spiritual race, you have
to first handle the task at hand, the challenge staring you right in the
face—and you'll never be able to handle them in your own strength.

Giving vs. Serving

Some of you are probably wondering what the *WIIFM* (What's In
It for me) factor when it comes to serving heaven's way. Since you're
giving so much sacrificially, there's bound to be a nice reward on
the other end—right? Yes ... and no. Let's look at this for a minute.

Bondhood is a tremendous act of maturing faith. We'll never be
able to serve heaven's way as long as we insist on clinging to spiritually childish attitudes (and WIIFM definitely qualifies as a childish
attitude).

Giving is a virtue similar to serving. Giving is also an act of
maturing faith. Both come with specific rewards, but it's important that we understand the huge difference between serving and
giving—and the different rewards that they each generate.

When we give (or sow)—whether it's money, material goods,
our time or our talents—we literally take something that belongs
to us and we release it for the purpose of advancing the work of the
Kingdom of God in some way. The scriptures teach very specifically

that such actions will be rewarded with a commensurate return (or harvest) in this life (see 2 Cor. 9:6–8, Prov. 11:24; 22:9, Lk. 6:38, Gal. 6:7–9). The key is that whatever is given actually *belongs to us*, therefore whatever harvest our giving produces also *comes back to us*.

However, when it comes to serving heaven's way, as bondservants we *no longer own* what's being given. As slaves we consider ourselves merely as part of God's inventory, part of his ransomed estate. When we give of ourselves in Godly serving, we're merely taking something that belongs to God (in this case, us) and using it the way he wants it used. Any return on that type of service goes straight to God, *not to us*.

Think of it this way: let's say I take $100 of my own money and invest it in the stock market. Within a month, the stock price goes up and my $100 investment is now worth $150. The $50 increase comes directly to me and I can use it as I choose.

But suppose *you* give me $100 of *your* money and ask me to invest it for *you*. When the stock price goes up, the increase on that $100 goes to *you*—even though I invested it for you. The clear difference is not in who invested the money, but in who actually owned the money that was invested.

Bondhood is an investment in the Kingdom of God and its gains go towards building and expanding the Kingdom of God.

A Servant's Reward

Still, the scriptures teach that godliness is profitable and has rewards—some which we'll receive in this life, others in the life to come. Most of the rewards that we'll get from serving we'll receive in the life to come. However, we'll receive two particular rewards in this life.

The first of these is joy. In the same way the Greek word *agapao* means unconditional, changeless love, the Greek word *chara* means unconditional, changeless joy. This type of joy is a "finish line" product. It consists of peace, wholeness, and celebration. This joy centers on God's finished work and eternal victory for a specific situation. *Chara* reaches into the future—where all of the battles are finally over—and brings that celebratory atmosphere into our present . . . regardless of what present difficulties exist.

The believer who successfully learns to serve heaven's way has this type of rarified joyous atmosphere deposited right in the middle of their souls—if they dare receive it by faith! Both Old and New Testaments call it "fullness of joy"—a type of wonderful, vibrant sensation that only flows from the presence of God (see Matt. 25:21; Psa. 16:11; Jn. 15:11). Once we receive this joy, we'll also experience an accompanying sense of rest—a soft breeze and refreshing mist traveling through our souls.

The second reward we get in this life is increased responsibility (see Matt. 25:21, 23). The scriptures clearly say if we show ourselves to be faithful over a few things, our responsibilities will be increased or expanded. Being given more work doesn't really sound like my idea of a reward, but it's the equivalent to receiving a promotion on your job or graduating from high school or college.

As we rise higher in our maturity level in spiritual things, God releases even greater levels of his grace, virtue, and wisdom to accompany our new levels of responsibility. In the end we become vessels of honor, fit for the Master's use and service.

Pace Yourself

Undoubtedly, the lives that have shined the brightest throughout history are the lives of people who found and walked the path of bondhood. People like Mother Teresa, Martin Luther King Jr., Mohandas Gandhi, Chiune Sugihara, David Livingstone, William Wilberforce, and Albert Schweitzer stand out as examples of people dedicated to this kind of serving lifestyle. I'd like to leave you with a few final key thoughts before we move on to the next chapter.

Most likely, you'll find that bondhood will never quite fit comfortably with your own humanity. There's always going to be some level of internal resistance. This resistance comes from our carnal nature, sometimes referred to as "the flesh." It's selfish in every way imaginable and will resist all efforts to walk in bondhood. Don't feel condemned or defeated by this resistance; it's as natural as the force of gravity, but, like the force of gravity, it can be overcome.

The primary approach to gaining victory over our internal resistance will come through the two Servant's Keys we discussed earlier, but we'll also have to train our flesh to submit to our spirit—another ongoing learning and living process.

Additionally, it's been my experience that the challenges to serve heaven's way will increase in scope and intensity as time progresses. The assignments to serve tend to get tougher, not easier. The course gets more challenging as we get closer to the finish line, but the advances of the Kingdom are greater.

Jesus' life was a clear example of this same pattern. His first act of service was to turn water into wine at a wedding in Cana. His final act of service was to turn sinners into sons on the cross at Calvary. His first act of service involved pouring out someone else's water; his final act of service involved pouring out his blood. His first act of service cost him his anonymity, his final act of service cost him his life. So don't faint in your minds or grow weary in serving. Remember, God gives more strength, virtue, and grace as the demands of bondhood grow greater.

Dr. Martin Luther King Jr. said the following words: "Everybody can be great, because anybody can serve. You don't have to have a college degree to serve. You don't have to make your subject and your verb agree to serve. You don't have to know the second law of thermodynamics in physics to serve. You only need a heart full of grace . . . a soul generated by love."[14]

Epilogue

I pray and sincerely hope that you've been blessed by something in this chapter. It's my desire to see you grow—to see you break free of the Lost in Faith Experience. Please remember that the anchor tenet encourages you to Pace *Yourself*—not your spouse, your child, a relative, friend or associate. Even though others can benefit from the teaching in this chapter, please focus on learning, growing, and implementing this teaching in *your own* life. Don't lose sight of the fact that this book is written for your benefit *first*.

World War II was one of the most difficult times in modern history. American soldiers on the frontlines of battle were faced with incredible hardships. Survival required them to be as prepared as possible, and to be caretaker for the soldier fighting next to them. Responsibility for your fellow soldier became a battle cry. Stories of heroism from this war still inspire us today.

Alma Bazel Androzzo was an unknown songwriter from Arizona who was living in Chicago during this time. Wanting to boost national morale, she wrote the following chorus, which became a theme for the service members overseas. It also fits in well with the principles of serving heaven's way:

If I can help somebody, as I pass along,
If I can cheer somebody, with a word or song,
If I can show somebody, how they're travelling wrong,
Then my living shall not be in vain.

If I can do my duty, as a good man ought,
If I can bring back beauty, to a world up wrought,

If I can spread love's message, as the Master taught,
Then my living shall not be in vain.[15]

Pace Yourself.

WASTE YOURSELF —PART 1

Freedom from mental and emotional bondage

Canst thou not minister to a mind diseased,
Pluck from the memory a rooted sorrow,
Raze out the written troubles of the brain,
And with some sweet oblivious antidote
Cleanse the fraught bosom of that perilous stuff
Which weighs upon the heart?[16]

In Madrid, they're referred to as *Gallinejas*. The Polish use them to make *Kishka*. The French outshine everyone with a delicacy called *Les tricandilles*. In Southern Illinois we simply called them *chitlins*. No matter how you prepare them or what you call them, these dishes all have one thing noticeably in common—they smell. More specifically, they stink.

Chitlins come from pigs, and their distinct smell results from their function while inside the pig—they contain the pig's excrement. From that, it shouldn't take a lot of imagination to figure out what they smell like. Still, many people consider the satisfaction they get from the sharp-tasting meat to be worth the trade-off of the unpleasant odor.

People come up with all kinds of ways of preparing chitlins in order to stifle the smell. This includes various methods of boiling, sautéing, steaming, as well as smothering in all kinds of herbs, spices, and sauces. Yet, in spite of the most imaginative culinary tactics, the resilient stench still manages to drift through.

As bad as the smell is, the more serious concern is the harmful bacteria that can reside in the linings of the meat. The most dangerous of these are E. coli and Salmonella—both known causes of serious illness and even fatality. The process of *cooking* chitlins is really a matter of taste, but the process of *cleaning* chitlins can literally be a matter of life and death.

As I approached this chapter, I felt that the chitlins analogy would be the ideal diving board into what I consider the number one cause of the Lost in Faith Experience—the *Entrenched In Stench* Fury. This Fury deals with the issues associated with mental and emotional baggage. I consider it the most all-encompassing of the five Furies for one simple reason: it's everywhere.

From the prayer-altar to the pulpit, from the new believer's class to the mission field—wherever you look, you'll see people of faith wrestling with some form of mental or emotional baggage. When I refer to mental and emotional baggage, I'm specifically talking about any disposition, attitude, behavior, or outlook that trips up our efforts to live the abundant life promised in the scriptures.

Abundant life touches every aspect of living. It includes spiritual, physical, mental, and emotional health. It also means having enough material means to provide for ourselves as well as to share generously. From fulfilling relationships to inner peace—it covers everything that contributes to our well-being.

Mental and emotional baggage might allow you to experience life on this level occasionally, but it won't let you live there permanently.

Intangible Waste

I've come up with my own term for this type of mental/emotional baggage: *soul trash*. Soul trash is the hard-to-scrape-off intangible residue we pick up from experiences in life that traumatize us. It's those issues that remain unresolved, indisposed, or both.

Soul trash is the floating chaff that blocks our airway when we try to breathe deeply from the enjoyable parts of life. It clutters the hallways of our minds, restricting or redirecting our movements at every turn. No matter how well hidden, soul trash produces enough unsettling clutter to keep us from being or becoming whole.

Like a camouflaged hummingbird nest, soul trash is seldom obvious. It's usually not the first thing that jumps out when we meet someone or when they meet us. Even so, though it lies quietly beneath our surface, soul trash will eventually let others know that it's there. In its own impeccably inopportune time, it will announce itself through various expressions of anger, fear, coldness, self-centeredness, and the like.

The Entrenched in Stench Fury is the toxic radiation produced by all the soul trash we accumulate as we go through life. It makes us leak uncontrollably.

Getting back to our chitlins analogy, it would be easy to compare the unhealthy dangers of eating poorly cleaned chitlins with the unhealthy dangers of mishandling soul trash. Both can make you sick . . . or kill you.

In his landmark book, *None of These Diseases*, Dr. S.I. McMillen lists over fifty diseases (including ulcers, high blood pressure, heart attack, and kidney disease) that can develop from harboring these detrimental, negative emotions.[17] The correlation is clearly there—but that's not what I had in mind.

An even more obvious comparison would be between the unpleasant *smell* of chitlins and the stench that comes from a bad attitude. You've probably heard someone say, "That person's attitude stinks!" Motivational speaker Zig Ziglar coined the phrase, "Get rid of your stinkin' thinkin.'" No matter how we try to cover up a bad attitude, like a pungent bowl of chitlins, the unpleasant smell always punches through. Again, the correlation is there, but that's not what I had in mind either.

My choice to use the chitlins illustration is based in anatomy. The meat used in making chitlins actually comes from the intestines. The intestines are located in the area of the body that also includes the kidneys, pancreas, and genitals. These organs are commonly referred to as the *loins*.

Lessons from Loins
The loins are responsible for *reproduction* as well as *waste removal*. The processes that take place within the loins are fascinating. For example, the lower intestine alone carries trillions of bacteria that aid in the digestion of food. This environment, called the intestinal flora, protects the rest of the body against poisons or allergens we eat, inhale, or somehow get into our bodies.

Exposure to many of the bacteria found in the intestinal flora would normally harm us. However, within the intestinal barrier, they safely break down the contents that enter the body. They help us absorb what's useful and get rid of anything unneeded. This amazing environment determines whether our reproductive, digestive, and immune systems function properly. It's really the cornerstone to the body's survival. No doubt, this is why Hippocrates concluded that "All disease begins in the gut."

A well-known expression regarding the loins is to "gird your loins." This phrase dates back to the nomadic tribes that dwelt in the Middle East thousands of years ago. They wore layers of loose-fitting clothes that protected them against the regional heat and winds. However, if someone needed to move about quickly, they would gather their robes around their waist and secure them with a thick sash or leather belt. This act became known as "girding your loins."

During times of warfare or conflict, they would gird additional layers of leather material tightly around their loins for extra protection. To "gird up one's loins," then, means a person is about to prepare for higher levels of activity or provide greater protection against danger.

In a letter written to a handful of fledgling churches in Asia Minor, the apostle Peter urged them to "gird up the loins—*of your mind*" [emphasis added] (1 Pet. 1:13). This novel phrase was a reminder to them to do three things:

1. Focus on activities that are productive, not wasteful.
2. Make sure that their resources for spiritual productivity are healthy.
3. Provide additional protection for upcoming hardships.

All three of these tasks involve a single common area of human nature: *the mind*.

The Mind

In most instances in scripture, the word "mind" refers to the human soul. Technically, the mind is only a part of the soul. Certain functions of the mind, soul, and spirit overlap—they interface but don't integrate. Let's look at the main differences between them:

Ten Primary Operations of the Soul[18]
1. Collects Sensory Information (What I Perceive)

2. Memory (What I Recall)
3. Intellect (What I Think)
4. Emotion (What I Feel)
5. Passion (The Intensity Of My Feelings)
6. Outward expressions (What I communicate)
7. Place of Imagination (What I meditate on)
8. Will (What I Choose)
9. Birthplace Of Creativity (What I conceive)
10. Controls the body (What I do)

Ten Primary Operations of the Spirit
1. Is the wellspring of life
2. Communicates directly with God
3. The place of intuition
4. Seat of the conscience
5. Seat of moral awareness and understanding
6. The legitimate throne of personal government
7. Lodging place for God's presence
8. The birthplace of faith
9. Interacts with the world of supernatural/spiritual realities
10. Inspires (gives life to, animates) the soul & body

The two Greek words most often translated "mind" in the New Testament are *psuche* (soul) and *pneuma* (spirit). However, when Peter introduces the phrase "gird the loins of your mind," he uses neither of these more common terms. Instead, he uses the word *dianoia*—and not by accident. The word *dianoia* applies to a very specific process of the mind. In fact, it has such a precise meaning that it rarely appears in the Bible—about thirteen times in all.

Dianoia is the same word Jesus used when a Jewish scholar asked him which commandment was the most important. Jesus replied, "to love God with all of one's heart (or spirit), all of one's soul, all of one's mind (*dianoia*), and all of one's strength" (Mk 12:28–30). Since we've already identified the tasks of processing thoughts as a function of the soul (which Jesus also mentioned), then we need to understand why he emphasized this specific mental function.

Dianoia is the soul-centered process that *manages* the unhealthy thinking patterns that work against our faith. The theological definition of *dianoia* is "the consequential power of contemplation, understanding and reflection which leads to the perception of good thoughts, evil thoughts, imaginations, opinions or judgments."[19] It's a mouthful to be certain, but basically it's a specific thinking process that rearranges the contents of the mind.

When God declares "our thoughts aren't like his thoughts and our ways aren't like his ways" (Isa. 56:8), he looks to the *dianoia* process to realign our thoughts and ways to his standards.

The Greeks gave us the word *dianoia,* and Peter gave us the expression *"gird up the loins of your mind."* Let me give you a phrase that represents a powerful spiritual anchor to help resolve and dispose of soul trash—Waste Yourself.

Waste Yourself

Waste Yourself is the third anchor of this book. It's the prescription for purging soul trash from our pasts, as well as disposing of the soul trash that comes at us throughout the day. The Waste Yourself anchor helps you cut the ties between the pain from your past, the possibilities of your present, and the promises for your future.

Things That Go Bump n the Spirit

Truthfully, every person reading this book is dealing with soul trash on some level (whether we realize it or not). All of us have had traumatic experiences that have changed us for the worse. Things that go *bump* in the soul. In many cases we don't even know that anything damaging has happened. In fact, by the time we realize we've sustained some kind of emotional or mental damage, the harmful roots from the incident have already started growing in the soil of our personality.

It's remarkable that we could be emotionally or mentally traumatized, yet unaware of it. This reminds me of an experience I had just out of college. I was driving my sister's sports car when the brakes went out and I ended up in the path of an oncoming truck. The collision was sudden and violent—my head smashed against the windshield and I was thrown from the car onto the shoulder of the road. My body was sprawled on the pavement with lacerations and swelling on my face and head, pieces of glass embedded in my forehead, and deep-tissue bruises throughout my body—but *at the time I thought I was fine.*

My mind played out a scenario in which I thought I had escaped the accident with virtually no injuries. The doctor later explained that the impact of the collision sent me into instant shock, which caused a temporary misalignment between my body and mind. My perception of what had really taken place was completely out of focus. This is what happens when we experience trauma to the soul.

The Shocking Truth about Sin

Sin collides violently with God's purposes for our lives. It traumatizes the soul. Every sinful experience sends our soul—to some degree—into a state of "shock." The result is an instant misalignment of our spirit, soul, and body. In some cases our conscience may let us know it's been violated, but we rarely fully understand the degree of the shock to the unseen parts of our nature.

Sometimes the simplest, most innocent-looking experience can be the entry point for devastating soul trash. For example, something as well-meaning as a surprise birthday party can startle us, depositing the small seeds of fear and anxiety. Over time, these seeds can grow into oak tree-sized phobias that strike at our mental and emotional health. Soul trauma from everyday experiences like this can develop into crippling problems we grapple with for a lifetime.

I don't want anyone confused by my use of the term "sin." The term *sin* covers both our willful disobedience to what we think God wants, as well as the general *fallen* state of creation. Sin has caused nature to collapse on itself involuntarily (as best seen in the diseases, natural disasters, pain, and calamity in the world). In contrast, voluntary sin (our individual choices to disobey or disregard what God wants) represents a dangerous, personal declaration of independence from God.

When we sin voluntarily we also choose to step away—to distance ourselves—from God. When we step away from him, we move away from the resources we need to be healed and liberated from the damages of soul trash.

Melva Henderson says that when we separate ourselves from God we immediately move into lack.[20] If we're to recover fully from the trauma of sin, we have to receive healing and restoration from God's resources. We can't benefit from these resources if we're steadily running from them.

The scriptures infer this fact with the question: "shall we continue in sin that grace may abound?" The implied answer is "no," because when we steadily move away from God we diminish our chances of ever completely recovering from the devastating effects of soul trash.

Waste Yourself 101

"He has sent Me to heal the *brokenhearted*, to proclaim liberty to the captives, and the opening of the prison to those who are *bound*" [emphasis added] (Isa. 61:1).

Brokenhearted . . . captive . . . bound.

Soul trash causes brokenness, isolation, silence and darkness in lives that were designed to shout and glisten. Its negative impact can poison a life.

Most people make the mistake of thinking this kind of long-term damage only comes from the more intense types of traumatic experiences (violent assaults, molestation, physical and verbal abuse, etc.). However, studies show that most soul trash actually comes from manageable incidents we simply *mismanage.*

Over ninety percent of our soul trash begins with trivial misunderstandings and offenses over things common to everyday living. In time, these slight scratches become oozing, open wounds—mainly because our constant picking at them causes infection rather than healing.

In fact, many people within the faith community look after these personal wounds, not in order to heal them, but rather to keep them raw enough to display before others in their ugliest light—a reminder to everyone of how badly the person feels they've been mistreated, violated, or victimized. They use their emotional scars as icebreakers, conversation starters. They choose to make room in their lives for fear, anger, or shame, disregarding the shackles that come with this choice.

It's All in Your Mind

Let's talk about the mind for a moment. Sometime during your childhood you probably learned that each one of us has our own unique set of fingerprints. The same is true of the mind—each one of us has a unique pattern for processing information—a *mindprint.* This mindprint contributes heavily to how we perceive things that happen around us. Whenever we receive information (through our five senses) we each focus on certain aspects of that information, while barely noticing other aspects. In other words, each of us sees things differently.

For example, suppose you and I go into the grocery store together to buy a gallon of milk. We walk into the building together, go over to the dairy section where the milk is displayed, pick the brand we want, walk over to the checkout counter, pay the cashier, walk out of the store, get into the car, and drive off. Even though we were together the entire time, our experiences were actually completely different.

For example, perhaps when we first walked in I may have noticed a big wad of gum stuck on the floor—something you may not have even seen. You may have spotted a sign that said "tomatoes on sale for 58¢ a pound"—a sign that I didn't even notice. At the checkout stand, I may have browsed a sports magazine while you may have thumbed through *TV Guide*. You may have observed a butterfly tattoo on the cashier's wrist, which I may have completely missed. While walking back to the car I may have watched a hawk circling lazily in the air, while you observed a couple in a dark blue mini-van having a heated discussion.

The fact is our observations of the world around us are never the same—in many cases, they're not even close! Accordingly, the information we store in our memory about an incident is never the same. No wonder when we recall an incident we both observed, our descriptions sound like two very different incidents—and they're *both* right!

On top of this, each of our minds has a unique way of encrypting the information it processes. Encryption is simply a unique formatting that makes information unreadable to anyone without the master codes and keys that make the information useable. In the same way your fingerprint is unique to you, your mind uniquely encrypts and decrypts the information it processes.

Not only are these encryption algorithms unique, but they change constantly. This is one of the reasons it's simply not possible to "read" someone else's mind. Even if you could somehow tap into some neurologic transmission wavelength and capture the information that someone else's mind was processing, it would still be incomprehensible because it would only make complete sense to the mind that created it.

One of the main functions of the mind is to combine new information it receives with old information that's already stored in your memory. The mind also references other parts of the soul (emotion, passion, imagination, etc,) and develops conclusions once everything has been processed and sorted. These conclusions are the basis for both our actions and attitudes.

To put it in even simpler terms, the mind's primary job is to *think*.

According to the National Science Foundation, the average person thinks about twelve thousand thoughts per day or five hundred thoughts per hour. A deeper thinker processes fifty thousand thoughts daily or a little over two thousand thoughts per hour.

Even when our mouths are closed, we're still engaged in what amounts to a non-stop internal conversation (my term for this is *mentalogue*). Psychological studies show that 95% of all these thoughts are *exactly the same as the thoughts from the day before!*[21] The repetitive nature of this mentalogue reinforces whatever perceptions we've already established. It defines our individual realities and cements our attitudes. Soul trash can dominate this repetitive, self-talk activity—and therein lies one of our biggest problems.

Waste Yourself 201

In order to understand how and why soul trash really influences us, let's take a closer look at what actually happens when we recall a memory. When we want to recall an incident from the past, we send out a mental command to pull up a record that's been stored in the vault we call our memory. This memory record contains the basic information about a specific event—as we perceived it.

The memory record passes through our emotional chambers, where an emotion (or several emotions) attach themselves to it (I define an emotion as a subjective feeling or state of mind that influences our physiology and behavior).

There are specific things about this memory record that attract certain emotions—I'll explain this in detail later. So by the time the memory actually arrives in our consciousness, we're really dealing with a lot more than just the basic facts of the incident. We're presented with what I call a *memory package.*

The emotions that come with this memory package will try to dominate your behavior. The degree to which they'll be able to do this will depend on their *intensity level.* If their intensity level is high, they'll probably dictate your behavior. If their intensity level is low, their influence on your behavior will be negligible.

The question is: what actually determines the intensity level of one of these particular emotions? Something I call the "passion factor." The passion factor sets the intensity level for these emotions based on two things: the *amount of time* you've spent meditating on that particular past event and *the nature* of these meditations.

The Romans used the term *metron* to describe this meditation process. *Metron* accounts for the method to determine the value of something, based on a value that's already established for something else.

For example, the average sixteen-ounce container of bottled water normally sells for about $1.00. However, in most American theme parks, the same bottle of water sells for as much as $5.00—five times more! Even though there's no real justification for the inflated cost, the operators of the theme park are able to manipulate prices at the park. Patrons of the park complain, but they still keep paying the high price.

In similar fashion, the values of the emotions that come with our "memory packages" are usually way out of proportion, due to overinflated intensity levels. The intensity of a person's emotions are determined by their perceived value of something related to a particular incident, balanced against their perceived value of their own worth. It follows that one of the most important questions in this *metron/meditation* equation is this: What do you think your life is worth?

The Greek philosopher Protagoras taught that *man* ultimately determines his own value, and thus sets the bar for the subsequent value of anything that happens during his life. Plato, a Greek philosopher who came after Protagoras, disagreed with this viewpoint and argued that only God could really define these values.

These two conflicting opinions converge at the intersection of Proverbs 23:7 and Proverbs 19:21. The first passage ("As a man thinks in his heart, so is he") seems to lean towards Protagoras' view. It suggests that man has some level of self-determination in the matter. However, the second passage ("There are many plans in a man's heart, nevertheless the Lord's counsel—that will stand") reminds us that man's plans—whatever they may be—may flourish for a time but will ultimately either conform with or fall before God's will.

Man's default point of view tends to amble through the halls of carnality. The word "carnal" refers to an ideology that places man's role as the dominant creature on earth at the center of all things.

The carnal view of life is overwhelmingly sinful—not because man is so inherently evil, but because carnality, at its core, regards the creature's opinions to be equal to God's. They're not.

It's this same kind of reckless thinking that got Lucifer into trouble—believing that the creature could be equal to (or even greater than) the creator. The main difference between man and Lucifer is that man is a *human* being, whereas Lucifer is an *angelic* being.

The Bible explains very clearly that the carnal mindset is antagonistic towards God and ultimately leads to self-destruction (see Rom. 8:6–8). It causes both deafness and blindness to the things that God says are important. The more we gratify the carnal mindset, the more difficult it becomes for us to perceive what God really wants. The meditation process plays a heavy role in developing our fixed mindset—whether carnal or godly. This is precisely why David, the great king, psalmist, and poet wrote: ". . . let the meditations of my heart be *acceptable* [italics added] in your sight, Oh God" (Ps. 19:4).

Let's take a minute and put the spotlight on the word "acceptable" from the previous passage. Some emotional expressions are acceptable and useful to God's purposes for us, while others are hostile to God's purposes for us. Even most negative emotions have an acceptable time, place, and manner for expression.

For example, it's acceptable to be angry if you walk into your teenager's room and find him watching pornography. There's an acceptable place to express emotions like guilt associated with having an unnecessary abortion, shame associated with having an extra-marital affair, despair associated with not being able to provide adequately for your family, bitterness associated with being slandered, fear or anger associated with being physically or verbally abused—the list is virtually endless.

You've probably heard about the dangers of choking one's emotions, of allowing your feelings to build continuously over time. John Sterling said, "Emotion, turning back on itself, is the element of madness." I'm not suggesting you repress your feelings completely, but I am suggesting you learn to express your feelings responsibly and release their energy properly.

When you learn to express these negative emotions at the right time, the right place, and in the right way, it helps you release the psychosomatic pressure created by a traumatic situation. However, these emotions become counterproductive to God's purpose for you when you continue to express them improperly or stifle them (to your hurt).

In times of trauma our emotions often serve as a buffer, an outlet, a crutch. But like most crutches, we're only supposed to lean on them briefly—*not* long-term, and certainly not for a lifetime. We've got a serious problem if we're still expressing these emotions *whenever* we think of a traumatic incident from our past—in some cases years or even decades later. We've got even bigger problems if these emotions are still strong enough to change our behavior.

Compare expressing an emotion whenever you recall a specific incident with grabbing a set of crutches whenever you think about the time you sprained your ankle as a kid. Neither action makes any sense, but life stops making sense when we don't deal with soul trash properly.

In a letter to a young pastor who struggled with feelings of inadequacy, low self-esteem, intimidation, and other forms of soul trash, the apostle Paul explains that the Spirit of God doesn't employ harmful emotions (like fear) on any ongoing basis, but rather helps us control these emotions by enabling us to walk in godly power, love, and mental soundness (see 2 Tim. 1:7). Let's look at a practical illustration of how this actually works in our lives.

The following "document" represents a memory. Please take a moment to read this "memory record" carefully.

This is a pretty straightforward account of the event, with very little bias or commentary added to it. When we want to remember this particular incident, this is the record that's pulled from the vaults of our memory.

Overtime, as we recall this incident *and meditate on it*, we start to add bias and commentary to the record itself. This commentary can consist of additional facts, conclusions, presumptions, or other information. So, as time goes by, when we recall the event we don't get the original record but the altered version that includes our commentary.

Think of this as you would a homework assignment. When you turn the original assignment in to your teacher, it's just a clean copy of your work. But when the teacher returns the assignment back to you, the paper usually has additional marks and comments on it. For

THE CAR ACCIDENT

I was backing out of my parking space at the grocery store when I suddenly heard a loud crashing sound and felt the entire car shake. I knew immediately that my car had been hit.

I looked back and saw a green pick-up truck jammed into the rear-end of my car. As the driver got out of his truck he yelled at me, "Why don't you watch where you're going before you pull right out in front of people?" I was very nervous as I got out to look at the damage. Thankfully, no one was hurt in the collision.

Still shaken up by the whole thing, I called AAA roadside assistance, and a tow truck was on the scene in less than 20 minutes. The police also came and took an accident report.

My car was in the shop for about two weeks, but when I got it back, it was as good as new.

Memory Record 1

example, there may be an actual grade somewhere on the paper (A, B, C, etc.), as well as other corrections or comments written on the assignment ("This answer is incomplete," "give more details," "Good job," etc.).

Here's an example of the same memory record with commentary added from a person's meditations.

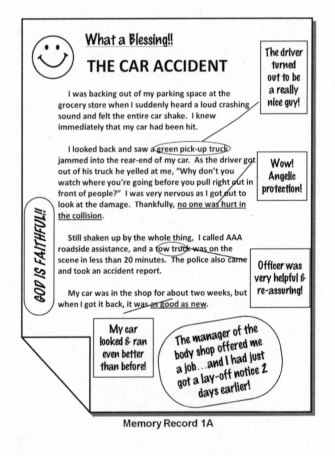

Memory Record 1A

As you can see, the commentary stands out from the original text. It's more noticeable and makes a big difference in how the memory record is viewed. Right off the bat you notice the words, "What A

Blessing!!" at the very top, next to the symbol for a happy face. This sets a positive tone, just at a glance.

The other added comments point out positive things that came from this incident, including an acknowledgement of divine protection, the fact that the car ran even better than before, an unexpected but timely job offer, and the benediction that "God Is Faithful!"

Because of the additional positive commentary that's been added to this memory record, whenever this person recalls this incident, they're going to feel uplifted and hopeful.

Now let's take a look at the same memory record with a different kind of commentary added.

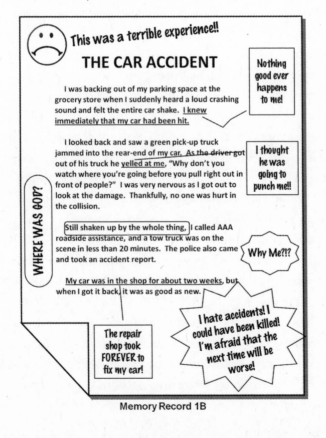

Memory Record 1B

Even at a glance, you can immediately see the difference between the commentary of Memory Record 1A and Memory Record 1B.

The first thing you notice is the "unhappy-face" symbol and the heading next to it that says, "This was a terrible experience!!" All the additional commentary supports this negative heading, highlighting one unpleasant thing after another. The two statements—"Nothing good ever happens to me" and "Why me?" establish a sense of victimization and ill-fate—a self-defeating combination if ever there was one. There's also emphasis on anticipated fear, pain, and frustration. It's no surprise that whenever this memory is recalled it's going to evoke very negative, unpleasant feelings.

It almost seems like the last two illustrations are talking about two entirely different incidents. However, we know they're the same. It's stunning to see how different a memory becomes once it's been modified by our meditation process.

Jesus addressed this very thing during a private conversation with his closest friends. He told them straightforwardly that: "The measure [of thought and study] you give . . . will be the measure [of virtue and knowledge] that comes back to you" (Mk 4:24 AMP).

This lesson about how the meditation process works drives home the fact that our meditation (on the one end) will always produce a reward or consequence (on the other end). If most of our meditation centers on carnal views, they produce passion fueled by worldly, cultural beliefs. However, when our meditations are centered around spiritual truths, they produce passion fueled by transcendent power from the Holy Spirit.

The commentary we add to a memory record through our meditations is the main part of the memory package that attracts emotion. Positive, optimistic comments attract positive emotions (like joy, hope, trust, etc.). Negative, pessimistic comments attract negative emotions (like fear, bitterness, anger, despair, etc.).

Neither godly nor ungodly forces have the privilege of actually adding any commentary directly to our memory—*only we* can do that. These forces, as well as other outside influences, can certainly plant suggestions in our minds, but ultimately our mental pen is the only instrument that has the right ink cartridge to add comments to our memory.

Any commentary in our memory that doesn't honor God is soul trash and needs to be disposed of. For every reason you can give for retaining such information, I can give you two compelling reasons not to:

1. Soul trash will disqualify you from receiving many of the blessings God has prepared exclusively for your benefit.
2. Soul trash will kill you prematurely.

Now that we've defined soul trash and studied its destructive nature, let's look at ways to get rid of it once and for all.

Chapter 6

WASTE YOURSELF
—PART 2

The nuts and bolts of moving beyond hurt and pain

*"All the art of living lies in a fine mingling of
letting go and holding on."*
—HAVELOCK ELLIS

If you've ever tried to change the rear brake pads on
a 2005 Mazda, then you know that some tasks just can't be done
without special tools. This is certainly true when it comes to treating
soul trash. It takes a specific set of tools to handle soul trash safely,
and a different set of tools to dispose of soul trash properly. This
section provides the tools to help you do both. Without them, our
efforts to deal with soul trash will only result in further contami-
nation—of us and others. Let's open the toolbox and get right to it.

The Waste Yourself Tool Kit
1. *Submit and Surrender to God* (James 4:7–8; Eph.6:11; 2 Chr. 15:2)
The first step in getting rid of soul trash is to submit and surrender to God. There are a lot of things you can do to bring temporary

relief to your situation, but this is where authentic recovery begins. Overlooking this step will only postpone your chances for permanent recovery. Submitting and surrendering to God consists of at least these three actions:

a. Acknowledging who God is (the divine creator and sovereign of all there is).

b. Acknowledging what God's proper role should be in your life (not an absentee dad or distant spiritual entity; but rather a present, active loving Father, an unfailing teacher, an absolute savior, a genuine friend and the only one worthy of worship).

c. Humbling yourself before God, making him your source and resource (remember, life operates at the highest level when you make God your bona fide, fulltime Lord—not just an emergency spare tire).

2. *Forgive and release anything and anyone connected to the incident* (see Matt. 6:14–15; Lk 6:37; Col. 3:13).
Forgiveness is a topic worthy of an entire book all to itself. Even if you were the target of unfair treatment, lies, slander, misuse . . . you must forgive and release it all.

Okay, you've tried to forgive (multiple times), but you're still stuck. You feel you need to work things out. If you could just get some things clarified you can have closure. Please highlight, underline, and memorize this statement: CLARITY AND CLOSURE NEVER PRECEDE FORGIVENESS—they only come afterward. Like the caboose follows the engine; like spring follows winter; like six follows five; so do clarity and closure follow forgiveness. Don't wait for clarity or closure to show up first, forgive *now* and let it go *now.*

There are two facts about forgiveness I urge you to remember, especially if you've tried and failed. The first is that forgiveness isn't a feeling; it's an act of faith. It's a choice. Faith heals feelings, but feelings can frustrate your attempts to forgive.

Don't be alarmed if you still feel anger, bitterness, or some other negative emotion towards someone even after you forgive them. No matter how strong these feelings are at the moment, they *will* change if you remain diligent to the *Waste Yourself* process. We are to forgive others freely, fully, and first because that's exactly how God forgives us (see Eph. 4:32). As you meditate on these truths, God's Spirit will begin to tenderize, fortify, and heal your heart. Eventually you'll learn to forgive as instinctively as you'd blink if someone blew into your eye.

The second point to remember is that unforgiveness really only hurts *one* person, while forgiveness really only helps *one* person. In both cases, that person is *you*. Your unwillingness (or inability) to forgive doesn't really restrict anyone but you.

Unforgiveness may strain your relationships—it may even destroy a relationship. Ultimately, however, the one it imprisons is *you*. Forgiveness releases you from this prison and moves your life forward dramatically.

Forgiveness requires us to guard our minds vigorously. In the early 90s, an R&B vocal group called En Vogue had a hit single that included the line, "free your mind . . . and the rest will follow." When we forgive and let go, it frees us—it's as if a chute opens, ejecting piles of soul trash out of our minds. When we've been wronged, it's easy to think about how we'd like to see justice, revenge, and vindication befall whoever hurt us. After all, they deserve it, right? Just remember, there's a price to pay for meditating on soul trash for any reason and in any form. The cost is an installment plan on unhappiness with an interest rate that keeps us in debt to pain.

There are plenty of excellent resources available on forgiveness. Let me recommend chapters three, twelve, and thirteen from the book, *Enjoying Your Journey with God* by Dr. Daniel A. Brown.

3. *Repent and Clear the Slate* (Psalms 139:23–24; Job 42:6; Joel 2:12–13; 2 Pet. 3:9)

We don't always see our need to repent for certain experiences—especially if we're clearly not the trespasser. After all, what sin is committed by a child who's molested by a demented uncle? Or what misconduct is committed by an employee who's the target of a boss's verbal outburst? The point we're missing is that sin leaves its stain on everyone involved. It marks the trespasser, the trespassed, and anyone just passing by.

We need to repent before God and ask him to cleanse the stain left by the troubling incident—for everyone involved. That stain can be as simple as a statement like, "I trusted that person and they let me down. I'll NEVER let that happen to me again!" This may sound like a harmless, fitting response, but in their *Breaking Free* program, Joel and Joanna Alvardo point out that this attitude can become a harmful inner vow that later grows into a spiritual stronghold in your life.[22]

This could be the seed that keeps you from trusting others—including God. These are the kinds of things that create pinholes in our souls. They make the invisible leakpoints that allow the warmth of life to leak out, leaving in its absence a place where love grows colder and colder.

Psalms 139:23–24 captures the essence of our need to repent perfectly: "Search me, O God, and know my heart; test me and know my anxious thoughts. Point out anything in me that offends you, and lead me along the path of everlasting life."

4. *Change the Filter* (Psalms 19:4; Proverbs 4:23; 2 Cor. 10:5; Phil. 4:8)

Our thoughts are often the unwitting caretakers of soul trash. It's critical to know which thoughts are helpful and which are harmful.

It's not always clear. To help remove the guesswork, I'm presenting Philippians 4:8 (I call it the P-48 filter). Whenever I feel spiritually lethargic, I can normally trace the cause to what I'm thinking.

Upon a genuine self-examination, I usually discover my mental filter has become dirty. A dirty filter = a dirty mind. When this happens, I simply switch to the P-48 filter and that usually fixes the problem.

The P-48 filter gives us clear direction on whether a thought is permissible or prohibited. Just as there are nine characteristics to the Fruit of the Spirit (Gal. 5:22) and nine expressions of the Gifts of the Spirit (1 Cor. 12:1–11), so there are nine spiritual screens that purify our thinking. Take a moment to study the list. I also suggest you write it down on a card and stick it in your wallet or purse: "Summing it all up, friends, I'd say you'll do best by filling your minds and meditating on things true, noble, reputable, authentic, compelling, gracious— the best, not the worst; the beautiful, not the ugly; things to praise, not things to curse" (Phil. 4:8 MSG).

Here's a list of all nine thought screens:

1. Is it *True? (note: Truth isn't just factual or a verified reality. Truth submits to God's purpose for man as seen from the cross.)*
2. Is it *Noble?*
3. Is it *Reputable?*
4. Is it *Authentic?*
5. Is it *Compelling?*[23]
6. Is it *Gracious?*
7. Is it focused on *the Best* or *the Worst?*
8. Does it celebrate the *Beauty* of a situation or it's *Ugliness?*
9. Does it inspire *Praise* or feel like a *Curse?*

Every imagination, meditation or thought needs to go through all nine screens. Anything that fails to make it past even one of these filters is dangerous and can potentially bring your life crashing to the ground. The epistle to the church in Corinth puts this in clear perspective when it says: "All things are lawful, but not all things are helpful. All things are lawful, but not all things build up" (1 Cor. 10:23 ESV).

There's no benefit to rummaging through the sewers to retrieve this putrid soul trash—it needs to be disposed of permanently.

5. *Don't Ever Let Blame Be a Focus or a Factor in Your Meditations* (see Matt. 7:1–5; Lk 6:37; Rom. 8:1, 14:3).

Blaming someone (or looking for someone to blame) is one of the biggest wastes of time for a true person of faith. It's a smokescreen straight from hell. You've probably heard the phrase "the blame game." Remove the "b" from the phrase and you'll see it for what it truly is—"the lame game"! The "lame game" will keep you crippled and weighted down with soul trash issues that push you further and further away from real liberty. Blame expands the size of the pinholes in your soul.

You should also avoid all forms of judging, finger-pointing, or condemning others. Romans 8:1 says, "There is no condemnation to them that are in Christ." Since God isn't condemning us, then we shouldn't be condemning anyone else. Judging and criticizing reveals more about what's wrong with you than with someone else. A judgmental spirit is the trademark of a person who walks in pride and is still trying to prove their own worth before God (and falling woefully short).

6. *Don't Make Presumptions* (see Num. 15:30; Deut. 17:12; Ps. 19:13).

A presumption is an unproven attitude or belief based on a probability, assumption, or likelihood. The presumption might be proven true later—but until it is, don't rely on presumptive thinking. Presumption and blame are separate off-ramps to the same dead end section of thinking.

Sometimes we feel we're being open-minded when we consider all the "presumptive possibilities" of a situation. However, most presumptions lie outside the safety zones of fact or forgiveness.

Presumptive thinking is like filling your gas tank with salt water and then wondering why your car won't run. Presumptions hamper your ability to think with the spiritual clarity that discerns God's purposes in a situation. Ultimately, presumptions create pinholes that siphon off our joy and cause our relationships to wither on the vine. The Bible gives us this strong warning and admonition about presumption: "Keep back your servant also from presumptuous sins; Let them not have dominion over me. Then I shall be blameless, And I shall be innocent of great transgression (Ps. 19:13).

7. *Wheat and Tares Strategies*

Tares are destructive (often co-dependent) people who are part of your family, your inner-circle, or connected to your household in some way. A tare could be a child, parent, sibling, spouse, or some other type of relative. A tare could also be a friend who's like a member of the family. Wheat and tares come up together, however, it's a tragic mistake to treat them the same.

Tares typically have self-destructive habits which dominate their lives and can bleed into your life if you allow it. Tares disrupt your peace and your progress. If you let them, tares will tear you down. They'll even conflict with who God has called you to be and what he has called you to do. If it reaches that point, you've got to make some serious decisions if you want your life to continue moving forward.

The familial nature of the relationship creates a special challenge when dealing with these people. Just as Satan tried to use the bond of the familiar scriptures to confuse Jesus while in the wilderness, tares will try to use the bond of relationship to put you into a wilderness of confusion and indecision. The relationship can distract from who *you* are and cause you to forfeit who you might become.

Here's a set of guidelines to help you plot a godly, victorious course when dealing with these unhealthy relationships. Let's start by looking at the following passage in which Jesus gives us some direct perspective about these matters:

> Don't think I've come to make life cozy. I've come to cut—make a sharp knife-cut between son and father, daughter and mother, bride and mother-in-law—cut through these cozy domestic arrangements and free you for God. Well-meaning family members can be your worst enemies. If you prefer father or mother over me, you don't deserve me. If you prefer son or daughter over me, you don't deserve me. (Matt. 10:34–37 MSG)

I've been in church my entire life, but I can't ever remember hearing a sermon or message taught from this passage. In fact, most pastors I know won't touch this passage with a ten-foot pole, because it implies separation within the family unit.

Our congregations spend a lot of time building up the idea of "family," and rightfully so. Many churches have mission statements that emphasize they're a family-oriented church. So the suggestion that certain family ties might need to be severed scares most pastors half to death. Ministers preach and teach all around this eight-hundred pound gorilla topic. The most common message from the pulpit about the subject is that believers should be patient, prayerful, and willing to placate or otherwise appease a person who's destroying their own life and the lives of others—all in the name of "love."

The patient and prayerful part I can go along with; however, believing that you should placate or appease any relationship that doesn't honor God or his purpose for you is a deceptive lie. It's a tactic designed to make you "double-minded"—perpetually conflicted by two seemingly irreconcilable values. This is nothing more than a well-devised scheme to keep you from living life at its fullest!

Here are some practical, spiritual steps to help you deal with the tares in your life.

a. Meditate on passages like Jeremiah 29:11, Ephesians 2:10, and Psalms 103 to establish a sense of your value in God's sight, as well as your place in his scheme of things. Let the word of God remind you who you are and your indispensable value!

b. Pray for wisdom and clarity as you move ahead (see Jas. 1:5–8).

c. Admit to yourself that the relationship doesn't honor God and take ownership of your role in participating with this (see Matt. 10:37).

d. Decide what's most important to you—honoring God or honoring the person (i.e. being intimidated) in this unhealthy relationship (see Acts 4:19, 5:29).

e. Decide what's more important to you—pursuing your eternity-touching, God-given purpose for being on earth, or protecting your time-dated, fleeting relationship with this person (see Lk. 9:59–62).

f. Ask yourself this tough question: "What would I be doing and how would I conduct my affairs if this problematic person wasn't part of my life" (see Rom. 14:12)?

g. Based on your answers to C, D, and F, establish a new set of boundaries for interacting with this person—boundaries that protect what you've determined to be your priorities and purposes (see Heb. 12:1–2). Write these set of boundaries on paper and review them several times daily (this is a *very important* step).

h. Remember that you're accountable for your life and *your* choices—not for anyone else's.

i. If possible, have a conversation with the person; something like this: "I've been thinking about my life and what I feel God has placed me here on the earth to do. I don't believe that our relationship brings glory to God or honors God's purpose for my life. It conflicts with what I believe in. Specifically, here are the things about our relationship that strike me as being the biggest problems." Then lay out each point.

j. Don't be surprised if they won't sit down and talk with you—remember, you're probably dealing with an adult who acts like a child. Make sure that you don't behave like a child in response. If they won't discuss the matter, then write them a letter, send them an email, text them—try to communicate by any means available. If communication isn't possible, don't let that stop you. Whether you talk with them or not, stick with your decision and start interacting with them based on the new boundaries you've set for the relationship. For further reading on setting healthy boundaries in your relationships, I suggest the book, *Boundaries*, by Dr. Henry Cloud and Dr. John Townsend.

k. Please don't think this is going to be easy. It sounds simple just reading these steps in this book, but it can be extremely difficult (I know from personal experience as well as counseling many people through these steps). It's tough, but it's worth it—and it works.

l. Be prepared to deal with tremendous emotional pro-
    test—from the other person as well as within yourself.
    Most likely, your emotions will resist any change—at
    least initially. Don't give up; it's simply part of the process.
    Read and meditate on the following passages, they'll help
    you get through this stage: John 16:33, 2 Timothy 3:12, 1
    Corinthians 15:57–58.

**8. *Don't take things personally or allow yourself to get offended*
(see Isa. 53, Matt. 26:57–74, 72:15–65; Heb. 12:1–29).**
I'm sure you've heard the term "theology"; it's the science of God. I'd
like to introduce a new term to you: *meology* (pronounced 'MEE-
ol-uh-jee'). Meology is the science of me, myself, and I. Actually,
meology is more of an illness than a science. It's the basis for most
offenses.

We get offended mostly when we fix our eyes on ourselves.
Men are often offended when they think they're being disrespected.
Women are more likely to get offended when they feel they aren't
given the proper consideration in a matter.

The key to reversing the problem of being touchy and easily
offended is found in four things:

a. Die to yourself (dead people don't get their feelings hurt).
b. Refuse to pamper, make allowances, excuses, or justify your
    offended feelings and behavior.
c. Repent and reject offense on the spot.
d. Study how Jesus dealt with offenses, particularly his exam-
    ple of suffering for mankind's sins.

Overcoming an offended heart isn't easy. It's a real fight—genuine
in-the-trenches spiritual warfare. Offense is a malignancy that
thrives in the darkness of self-pity and short-sightedness. Offense is

an unhealthy emotional shield, protecting the carnal thinking that blinds us, binds us, and pierces our souls.

If you're offended often, start setting aside at least half an hour each day (preferably a time you're not likely to be disturbed) to meditate and pray about the sacrificial life of Christ, and about your touchy nature.

Jesus' life is the blueprint for winning the battle with offense. He was lied to, abandoned, betrayed, beaten, spit on, humiliated, slapped, yet he endured without becoming offended. The creator of all things allowed himself to be disgraced, mistreated, humiliated, even crucified—at the hands of the very people he created! So you and I have absolutely no excuse. The writer of Hebrews put it like this: "When you find yourselves flagging in your faith, go over that story again, item by item, that long litany of hostility he plowed through. That will shoot adrenaline into your souls" (Heb. 12:3 MSG).

When we consider the humiliation he endured and the victory he won, it should help us remain humble and meek in the face of mistreatment, real or perceived. What's at stake are the victories that God wants to bring to and through us, victories that go far beyond the temporary humiliation we're experiencing. Winning the battle of an offended heart will lead to some of the greatest victories in your life.

9. *Avoid Dumpster Divers* (1 Tim. 5:13; 2 Thess. 3:11; 2 Pet. 2:17–19). Dumpster divers are people who love to stir up trash. They're the gossips, busybodies, and drama queens/kings who love meddling in other people's business. Most of their conversations include someone who's not in the room. They're the tabloid journalists of the faith community—always on the lookout for a rumor they can exploit or a story they can sensationalize at someone else's expense.

Take a look at how the Bible describes them: "There's nothing to these people—they're dried-up fountains, storm-scattered clouds, headed for a black hole in hell. They are loudmouths, full of hot air, but still they're dangerous" (2 Pet. 2:17 msg).

Dumpster Divers grieve the Holy Spirit by steadily slicing and segmenting God's family. They're divisive, dangerous, and contagious. Rebuke them, avoid them, and if necessary, delete them from your circle of friends.

10. *Victim or Victor* (Jn. 16:33; 1 Jn. 4:4, 5:4)

Whatever your particular challenge may be, you'll need to decide if you're going to be a victim or a victor. You can't be both. The victim chooses to make the trial the point of attention. Victims seek sympathy and restitution. Victors, on the other hand, have no time or need for these medications. Victors look to the cross—they keep their eyes on the prize and their feet on the path of undaunted purpose.

When you identify yourself as a victor, you must give up all the claims and sympathies that victims typically seek. When you identify as a victim, you forfeit the grace that can help you overcome your circumstances. By design and by nature, victims are *never* overcomers.

11. *Seasoning vs. Substance* (1 Kings 3:9; Ezekiel 44:23; Heb. 5:14)

Learn to identify and separate the *seasoning* of an incident from the *substance* of an incident. Seasoning is the term I use to describe the expressive but non-essential facts of an incident. It's the raised voice, the dramatic body language, and the expletives that smother the core message with its distracting tone and flavor.

Substance, on the other hand, is the term I use to define the core purpose an incident calls for. Substance is the *who, what, where, why, which, when, and how.* Think of substance as the steak and seasoning as the salt or pepper on the steak.

Seasoning appeals to our emotions and solicits an emotional response. If the seasoning is negative, it's a warning signal that a soul trash transfer is about to take place. When we feel the urge to react negatively, we must train ourselves to pause and remember that we're getting worked up over nothing more than a few *grains of table salt*. We're about to let a small condiment packet wreck our day, ruin a relationship, or potentially destroy our future.

12. *Turn Your Fast into a Feast* (Psalms 30:11; Isaiah 61:3; Zechariah 8:18–19).

For seventy years, the people of Israel held four separate annual holidays—or fasts—to commemorate four tragic events from the nation's past (see Zech. 8:18–19). The first fast observed Jerusalem's captivity to the Babylonians, the second fast was in remembrance of the burning and destruction of Solomon's Temple, the third fast observed the brutal murder of Gedaliah, Judah's governor, and the fourth fast commemorated the initial siege of Jerusalem by king Nebuchadnezzar.

These holidays were more like "horror-days," commemorated by fasting, mourning, sadness, wailing, grimness, and distress. Think about that! These people set aside four specific times in the year to make themselves miserable by reliving the pain of these horrible events! This sounds absurd, but many of us are guilty of similar behavior.

As the anniversary date of some tragic event from our past approaches, we become quiet, depressed, and brooding. The divorce date or the day a loved one passed. The date the home was repossessed and our belongings were put out on the streets. The date we were mugged, assaulted, or fired from the job unfairly.

Something in us suggests that it's fitting to observe these tough times with grief and sadness. Deception hides in the shadows of that kind of thinking. Fear generates this attitude.

For seventy years, God watched his people conduct these spiritually-anorexic memorials. They clearly had no clue to the damage they were doing to themselves. I believe God finally just got sick of it, or felt sorry for them. He sent an astounding word of prophecy to them. Here's what he told them:

> This is what the LORD of Heaven's Armies says: The traditional fasts and times of mourning you have kept in early summer, midsummer, autumn, and winter *are now ended*. They will become festivals of joy and celebration for the people of Judah. So love truth and peace. (Zech.. 8:19, NLT)

Wow! He actually told them to turn their "fasts" into "feasts" (I wish some of my pastors would have come up with this idea!). God told them to stop focusing on the tragic aspects of those events and re-direct their focus on his faithfulness to preserve them during those difficult times. He wanted them to focus on the future with its prom-ises, not the past with its pains.

God knew that this practice of grief-stricken fasting had no pro-ductive value to them. It was an emotional bookmark that kept them from moving forward—like a scratched vinyl record. The same holds true for us today.

Isaiah tells us that God has provided us special garments of praise to counteract the burden of heaviness. The choice is ours: we can marinate in misery, be held hostage by history, or we can cele-brate God's mercies. We can remain stuck, facing the tribulations from the past, or we can move ahead, facing the promises of the future.

Mental Instability

The tools in this chapter are meant to help us recover from emo-tional and mental problems that exist because of poor choices—either ignorantly or knowingly. These problems have spiritual roots that can be dislodged or healed. However, there are mental and emotional problems of a different nature that require a different approach. I'm specifically talking about genuine mental health conditions that affect behavior—the depression, bi-polar, phobias, anxiety, schizophrenia, and delusional disorders that can't be written off simply as someone having a bad day.

According to the National Institute of Mental Health, 26% of America's population is affected by some form of mental illness—that's one in four people.[24] Mental illness should carry no more stigma than cancer, kidney failure, or bronchitis—but we know that's not the case. The stigmas connected to mental illness are from the pits of darkness, based in fear and ignorance. They shouldn't exist in the faith community, but unfortunately they do. To our shame and through our ignorance, sometimes we make matters worse by labeling the mentally ill as demon possessed. They're not.

My grandmother once said that the mind is like a rock stuck in the ground—once it becomes dislodged it never quite fits back the way it was before. The pages of the Bible are filled with the stories of such people. We're inspired by the accomplishments of men like Elijah and Nebuchadnezzar, hardly considering that they were depressed prophets and deranged kings. If we met one of the authors of the imprecatory Psalms at a coffee shop, we'd likely do our best to avoid the ranting guy in the corner with the sour outlook on life.

Mental illness is a highly personal injury—not a contagious disease. In many cases, a broken mind can be traced to a broken dream . . . a broken home . . . broken heart. A lot of these cases result from deficiencies of esteem, love, respect, safety, etc.—many which go all the way back to a person's childhood.

Thankfully, God's grace doesn't abandon or ignore the mentally ill, nor should we. Our role as people of faith is to bring the powers of prayer, love, compassion, and understanding to support those who are suffering from mental illness as well as their families.

Prayer is a reliable approach to mental illness, but I also strongly advise seeking help from the medical community. Even if a person is completely healed by God's power—without the involvement of a doctor, I still suggest they follow up with a mental health professional to help them understand how they became mentally ill in the first place, and identify steps to prevent any recurrence.

If you're suffering from mental illness, don't be ashamed to take a break from life's routine and seek the help you need. Remember this well-known passage as you make the journey back to mental wholeness: "He makes me lie down in green pastures, He leads me beside quiet waters, He restores my soul" (Ps. 23:2–3 NLT).

Epilogue

It's my prayer that you've learned something and grown from reading this chapter. It's only natural to think about how the material can help people you know. However, before you share it, make sure you're starting to get the most you can from this chapter. This anchor urges you to Waste *Yourself*—not your spouse, your child, a relative, friend, or associate. Focus on learning, growing, and implementing this teaching in *your own* life. Please don't lose sight of the fact that this book is written for your benefit *first*.

It's heartbreaking to consider that millions of people in today's faith community grapple daily with the devastating problems of soul trash. They're entrenched in stench way over their heads. They're dominated emotionally and tormented mentally by anecdotal intangibilities—embalmed memories. Dead things. I believe that anything dead should be buried—*once and for all*. As Bishop Charles Blake says, "Nothing dead deserves a daily funeral."

It's time for you to be free. Your life doesn't have to be inhibited or defined by soul trash of any kind. Freedom *is* within your reach—the Kingdom *is at hand* for you—thanks to the mercy of God and the finished work of his only begotten son.

When it comes to seeing miracles of liberation in your life, don't sell God short. There's nothing too hard for him and he wants to restore your life to a state of complete spiritual, soulful, and physical health!

Take comfort and hope in the fact that God has more ways to liberate and restore you than there are grains of sand on the beach! He has more ways to heal you than there are raindrops in a thunderstorm. In addition, just as no one can stop every single raindrop from reaching the earth, no one can stop God's blessings of recovery from reaching your life and turning things around for you. Believe him!

The facts of your situations will try to *overwhelm* you.

The faults of your situations will try to *overtake* you.

The feelings of your situations will seek to *overpower* you.

However, if you're willing to *overlook* them,

Then God will *overturn* them,

And you can *overcome* them—by faith.

Waste Yourself.

Chapter 7

PLACE
YOURSELF

Courage and confidence

Like a bird that wanders from its nest is a man who wanders from his place (Pro. 27:8).

Most of us have snickered at the label on the mattress that reads, "Do Not Remove This Tag Under Penalty of Law." All jokes aside, the warning is actually aimed at manufacturers, not consumers. Manufacturers are legally bound to list all the materials used in their mattresses to show that the product complies with OSHA guidelines. The label also alerts consumers of any objectionable materials that go into making the mattress—particularly the padding.

Sometimes manufacturers try to cut corners, stuffing their mattresses with inferior materials like horsehair, newspaper, or even old rags. Once the seams are closed, it's almost impossible to tell what's really inside that mattress. But when field inspectors show up and rip open a few mattresses, the contents had better match the description on the label; otherwise someone's going to be hit with stiff penalties and sanctions.

Getting reliable information about the goods and services we use has been an ongoing concern, especially over the last half-century. Regulators want to see to it that products are safe, while consumers want to know that they're actually getting what they think they're buying. Labels help bridge the information gap.

Labels tell us the towing capacity of a pickup truck, the number of calories in an energy bar, the active ingredient in a bottle of cough medicine, and whether we should machine-wash or dry-clean the pullover we got on sale at Macys.

Unfortunately, labels aren't always precise, and sometimes they're blatantly dishonest. I learned this firsthand when I was around eleven. I ordered some "Sea Monkeys" in the mail based on an ad I saw in a comic book. The ad showed a happy family of marine creatures frolicking inside a fishbowl. The ad said, "We even show you how to teach them to obey your commands like a pack of friendly trained seals." At $1.25 (plus shipping), it was a deal I just couldn't pass up.

What I actually received in the mail was a small bag of dusty sand, at least that's what it looked like. I learned later that the sand also included sea salt and microscopic crustacean eggs. When added to water, the eggs hatched into brine shrimp that were so tiny, you needed a magnifying glass just to see them (fortunately, a cheap plastic one was included with the package). I never got the chance to see if the tiny "sea monkeys" could actually be trained to do tricks, because they only lived for about two weeks, after which they disappeared just as quickly as my $1.25 (plus shipping).

Labels help us feel organized, so we attach them to everything we can—including people. Consider the following personal labels: Olympic Gold Medalist. Welfare Mom. Struggling Musician. Kindergarten Teacher. Drug Dealer. Foster Child. Soccer Coach.

Each of these labels conjures up an image—some negative, some positive, some neutral. Sometimes personal labels are right on target, but they can also be misleading or flat wrong.

Take, for example, the label Doubting Thomas. This label is often pinned on people who have a skeptical outlook. If you recall, the label comes from Thomas' reputation as the lone doubter among Jesus' twelve disciples, based on his statement that he wouldn't believe Jesus had risen from the grave until he saw the nail prints in his hands and the spear wound in his side (see Jn. 20:24–29). With this in mind, look at how the following passage describes the other disciples' reaction to the same news:

> Then they (a few of Jesus' followers) went in and did not
> find the body of the Lord Jesus. And it happened, as they
> were greatly perplexed about this, that behold, two men
> stood by them in shining garments. They said to them,
> "Why do you seek the living among the dead? He is not
> here, but is risen! Then they returned from the tomb and
> told all these things to the eleven (disciples) . . . *and they
> did not believe them,*" [emphasis added] (Lk. 24:3–6, 9–11)

This passage clearly shows that initially, *all the disciples* were skeptical. However, Thomas is the only one straddled with the stigma of being a doubter. This brings us to the main subject of this chapter: the harmful labeling practices that take place within the faith community—a phenomenon I call the *Assimilation Mutation* Fury.

The Assimilation Mutation Fury is a one-size-fits-all approach to life and service within the faith community. It's a leading cause of the Lost in Faith Experience. The Assimilation Mutation Fury happens when people in the faith community have their individuality stifled in order to "fit in" with the flow of the rest of the congregation. It also occurs when a person's gifts and talents are used the wrong way or for the wrong reason.

This Fury pays little heed to God's plans and purposes for both the gift and the vessel—focusing instead on fitting this person into a template, making sure they match the other existing pieces in the group.

These actions are rarely carried out with any ill will in mind. Spiritual leaders genuinely want to help people serve in the church or faith groups they join, but sometimes the structure, format, or expectations of such serving comes at the cost of unintentionally stripping down the person's creativity and individuality. The result is a believer who's busy, but also unfulfilled . . . with little understanding why. The Assimilation Mutation Fury molds believers, but not necessarily in the image Christ had in mind.

Tag, You're It!

From the moment we become members of the family of God, someone wants to categorize us, to put us in the group they think we best fit, to stick a label on us. The labeling usually starts innocently enough with the faith community's round-peg nametags: Are you Protestant or Catholic? Baptist or Methodist? Charismatic or Pentecostal? Non-denominational or Ecumenical?

From there the labeling process intensifies, moving on to the faith community's triangular-peg practices: Should church music be performed by a traditional choir and organist, or a small group of singers accompanied by a rock-style band? Is it appropriate for people to dance, pray aloud, or wave their hands demonstratively during a worship service, or is it more fitting to remain as quiet, reserved, and composed as possible?

Finally, the labeling process dead-ends with some of the faith community's square-peg obsessions: When baptizing people in water, should the minister use the phrase "in the name of Jesus," "in the name of the Father, Son and Holy Spirit," or simply "according to their faith"? Is it okay for believers to smoke tobacco or drink alcohol in moderation, or should they abstain from these indulgences altogether? Should people of all races and ethnicities worship together if they have similar beliefs, or is it better for them to fellowship among their own social groupings?

The more fuss surrounding the labeling process, the more exclusive, separated, and clique-ish that particular group is inclined to be. Also, the more suppressive the group tends to be of individuality—spiritual or otherwise. There's simply no room for mavericks, the cadence of a different drummer, or anyone wearing a coat of many colors; after all, we're striving for uniformity around here.

In many cases this labeling process requires the believer to remove (or at least cover up) any previous identification tags, no matter how useful, accurate, or valid they may be. As we learned from our earlier mattress-tag example, messing with labels can have serious consequences.

When we join a church or faith group, people within the group are very happy to see us. They usually make a fuss about it, clapping and cheering their welcoming approval, and giving us a nice gift pen, a pad, and a voucher for a free CD.

Soon afterwards, however, the celebration gives way to the real work at hand: squeezing the new person into one of the old molds. They want our adjustment to the church's culture to go smoothly, and in many cases that means scrubbing away any existing identification marks.

This is usually where and how the Assimilation Mutation Fury starts to wipe away our uniqueness. The initial, "You're going to fit in great around here" is soon replaced by, "That's *not* how we do things around here."

The Assimilation Mutation Fury focuses mainly on surface-ware (the outward appearance that people like to notice). It works tirelessly to create its version of unity from the building blocks of uniformity. When the Assimilation Mutation Fury has run its course, your spiritual individualism is mostly hidden from view and your shiny new label is front and center. Congratulations, you're now officially one of us . . . or them (they both look so much alike, it's hard to tell the two apart)!

The Assimilation Mutation Fury has a clear message: to fully become part of the group, one must take on all the trademark characteristics of the group—*no exceptions!* There's no such thing as trying to "get in where you fit in"—either you comply with the group's existing mannerisms, or receive the left foot of fellowship.

We've all seen it. A gaggle of believers who all preach the same way, sing the same way, counsel the same way, teach the same way, pray the same way, dress the same way, look the same way. You get the picture.

In situations where people exercise the gifts of the Spirit, their unknown tongues sound noticeably the same, their words of prophecy seem to come forth in the same lilting or droning format, and their prayer and healing services follow the same assembly line patterns.

It's as if someone has taken the Photoshop blur tool and removed anything distinctive from the group. The level of uniformity can be stifling—enough, in fact, to make you blink hard, rub your eyes, and ask yourself, "Is this a worship service or a Stepford audition?"

The amount of sameness is staggering, especially when you consider how *different* God has made each of us! Any casual observer can see the incredible range of *everything* on our planet. The endless multiformity that surrounds us leads to a clear conclusion: God must love variety.

God created millions of different kinds of birds, flowers, fish and rocks. People come in all shapes, shells and shades. Even the most casual observer can see that when he made all of us, he didn't use an assembly line! God celebrates individuality. He sponsors diversity. Most importantly, he expects his body in the earth (i.e. the faith community) to be a brilliant representative of this diversity. Apparently not everyone got the memo.

Once a Thief Always a Thief

Your identity not only distinguishes you from other people, it also represents things you've accomplished and you've come to value. Little wonder that identity theft has steadily moved up the crime chart and is currently the number one consumer fraud concern worldwide.[25]

The US Federal Trade Commission says that 20 percent of all the cases they deal with involve identity theft—an astonishing number.[26] These theft cases are extremely costly and traumatizing. But identity theft isn't a new concept. Satan has been dealing in identity theft ever since he crashed the party in the Garden of Eden. He doesn't want you to come into the knowledge of who you really are and what you can accomplish. The Assimilation Mutation Fury is one of his most effective strategies to stop you.

Consider the tactics Satan used in the Garden of Eden. He told Adam and Eve that the knowledge they would gain after eating from the forbidden tree would make them like God. It was a textbook scam: he tricked them into overlooking the fact that they were already like God, created in God's image and likeness. The hoodwink continued as Satan diverted their attention with several outright lies; the biggest was telling them that gaining more knowledge would make them as powerful as God. People today still fall for this same scam.

There's a pervasive belief that increased knowledge is man's key to being more God-like. The truth is, we could combine all the knowledge of every person who's ever lived, multiply it by one trillion, and it wouldn't even move the dial on the "I'm-like-God" meter. God isn't who he is by virtue of what he knows. He's not a genius—he's *spirit*. Increasing your intelligence won't make you godlier.

Satan's goal is to get you out of the place God wants you to be by lying to you about every aspect of your life, starting with who *you* are. From the second you enter the world he starts to sow seeds along your path. He hopes they'll keep you from coming into the awareness of your complete identity.

To our shame, many of these seeds find ideal growing conditions inside the faith community. Believers unwittingly assist in the "relabeling" process that's part of the Assimilation Mutation. Their intentions are good. Their motives are usually pure. Unfortunately, the absence of malice doesn't make the outcome any less damaging.

Other Sheep, Other Folds

The Assimilation Mutation Fury creates an additional problem in the faith community—a false sense of spiritual enlightenment and an attitude of being better than other peer faith groups. We're right, they're wrong. We have a more mature understanding of the Word of God than they do. They're stuck in the spiritual horse and buggy era, we're moving in the fresh anointing of twenty-first century revelation! We're on a higher level than they are.

Yecch. Double yecch with a vinegar-face headshake. Here's how Christ sees the different groups in the faith community: "I have other sheep, too, that are not in this sheepfold. I must bring them also. They will listen to my voice, and there will be one flock with one shepherd" (Jn. 10:16, NLT).

In this passage Jesus speaks about different "sheepfolds" that would be established as his message spreads throughout the world. A sheepfold is a fenced enclosure where animals are grouped together for different reasons. Wealthy farmers own thousands of sheep, and it's impossible for a single shepherd to manage so many animals. The only practical solution is to divide them into different herds and place them under different shepherds. Even though the sheep are fragmented and spread out, they still belong to the same person.

Jesus looks at the faith community the same way. There are millions of denominations, church groups, independent faith-based organizations, religious sects, home study gatherings, and assemblies in the world today. They express their faith in different ways, but all who are born of his name and hold to his Word belong to God.

This isn't an endorsement for universalism or the "all paths lead to God" philosophy. Rather, it's a recognition of the variegated reality that Christ discussed before it ever happened (see Isa. 56:8, Eph. 2:11–19). Like it or not, everyone who has come into the faith community by way of the cross is part of the family of God.

The point to keep in mind when it comes to all of these groups within the faith community is this: Jesus anticipated their existence; it didn't seem to bother him, so we shouldn't let it bother us. In fact, the above passage from the Gospel of John says something that should help us understand this situation better: *"They will listen to my voice."*

Many of the differences among these groups within the faith community can be attributed to the fact that they've heard different instructions and they have different assignments. I compare this diversity to the way our kids clean the downstairs area of our home. Each one has a different area of responsibility. One cleans the kitchen, another tackles the family room, and another the guest bathroom. They each have a specific assignment, and they're assignments require different cleaning equipment. In the end, all the assignments work to achieve a single goal: cleaning the downstairs.

The faith community is similar to this. God dispenses different church groups to meet the various needs of humankind throughout the world. He's interested in more than just the city you live in or the church you attend.

For example, the denomination I grew up in was particularly gifted to serve effectively in hardcore, urban, inner-city environments. They've been effective in doing this all over the world.

Other groups are more effective in suburban environments, some in rural environments, some on college campuses, some in underdeveloped civilizations—the diverse assignments are too numerous to list. However, they have these things in common: they're all called, they all matter, they're all needed, and they're all different.

It's important that these groups retain their distinctive callings and their focus of ministry. They also need to appreciate particular mannerisms and styles that help make them effective in their calling. These are often the critical tools God has equipped them with to carry out their chief mission—whatever it may be.

They're all different parts of the same body. It goes without saying that they shouldn't be fighting each other—they all have a common enemy. More importantly, they all have a common Savior.

Rather than try to compete with each other, they should view each other similarly to the different branches of the military. Some groups are like the navy, some like the army, some like the marines, some like the Red Cross, and some are like the reserves. All are called for specific spiritual service and warfare.

Another area of foolish comparison involves different styles of worship. I was sitting next to a pastor at a convention not too long ago, and after the choir performed two songs, he leaned over and said, "I just don't care for this type of music. I want something lively and upbeat, something that makes my toes tap and gets the anointing flowing. I like the way *your* church worship team ministers. You folks really know how to praise God—without the brakes on! When

I come to church, that's what I want to hear; something that blesses me—not almost puts me to sleep!"

My reply to him is my sincere admonition to you. To begin with, praise and worship isn't done for our account or our benefit—it's offered up to God, and the only person who has to approve it or like it is him. I've been involved with worship music my entire life, and I understand the impact it can have in touching hearts and preparing the atmosphere for effective ministry. But let's never lose sight of who the real focus of the worship experience is.

Secondly, what many people call "anointed worship and praise" is often just a personal, cultural preference for a style of music. I've been in churches where people were "moved" by all styles of music—traditional hymns performed by large choral groups accompanied by full orchestras, country and western-style gospel sung by a family ensemble, quartet gospel, contemporary Christian music, black gospel, Southern gospel, gospel rock, gospel hip-hop—the list goes on and on.

It's good if a particular musical style touches someone and makes him or her draw closer to God. It's even better if the music touches God and causes him to draw closer to us.

The same can be said for styles of preaching or teaching. There are many different styles of preaching or teaching, but none of them have a corner on God's anointing or power. Neither God nor Satan is moved by whether we shout or whisper, sing ear-blasting gospel songs or tranquil traditional hymns, pray with loud agonizing groans, or simply pray to ourselves quietly.

The power of God and the "anointing" are released into the atmosphere by faith—not by a decibel level, a chord progression, or cultural flavor. Sometimes the Lord does prompt us to "cry out," and in those cases we should. But the way we express ourselves in worship is a matter between us and the Holy Spirit. Rarely do our outward expressions make a difference in releasing God's power in our lives. Noisier doesn't equal holier, nor does softer indicate greater reverence.

I connect with many groups within the faith community. It's also been my privilege to serve with several different churches, organizations, and groups. It's refreshing to see so many different ways of conducting God's work and expressing God's love.

I admit that I can't always relate to everything I've experienced, and I've found some of the things distracting at times. But I wouldn't trade one curious moment for the opportunities I've had to embrace the people who love God in other folds. The common denominator of the cross is ultimately greater than any organizational differences—a fact we would all do well to remember. The genuine love of God in a person's heart—no matter where they worship—connects us at the intersection of humility and wisdom.

We should keep these things in mind as we regard the diversity of the body. There's no Who's Who church register in God's view, and the question of "Which denomination or group represents the 'true church'?" is carnal foolishness of the highest order. There won't be a valedictorian chosen among the people who make it to heaven. Above all, we should remember that the faith community is diverse, but not divided.

Diversity without Adversity

Jesus' longest recorded prayer is in the Gospel of John. During this prayer, Jesus, thinking about his current and future disciples, makes the following request: "Father, make them *one* . . . just as *You* and *I* are *one*" [italics added] (see Jn. 17:11, 20–22).

About five years later, the same author (John) reveals even more complexity in God's nature when he explains, "There are *three* that bear record in heaven: the Father, the Word (or Son), and the Holy Spirit; *and these three are one*" [italics added] (see 1 Jn. 5:7).

For most people, the concept of "two being one" is puzzling enough—three being one is even more baffling. When we examine God closely, we see three distinct personalities: God the Father, God the Son, and God the Holy Spirit.

God exists as one being, yet coexists in three persons. The unity, or "oneness" of God hearkens back to the *Shema*—the passage from the *Torah* that puts forth the fundamental, monotheistic truth about God. It starts out like an epic poem, with the unforgettable opening: "Hear, O Israel: The Lord our God is one Lord!" (Deut. 6:4).

God doesn't want people confused about the fact that he's one God, so he brings it up when he first introduces himself, and repeats it throughout scripture. He's "one" in terms of his uniqueness (as in, there's *no one else like him*). He's also "one" in contrast to other polytheistic religious systems. He just happens to possess three distinct expressions of character. Confused? Hang in there; it gets clearer as we move along.

Tertullian, a second-century church father from Africa, is credited with being first to refer to God's nature as the Trinity (from the Latin word *Trinitas*). Even though the word "trinity" doesn't appear in the Bible, it's become one of the most recognized terms in Christian vocabulary or theology. Three persons in one essence; each personality completely integrated with the whole, each retaining their distinct individualities. Let's look briefly at some of the ways they actually differ.

1. By their *Names:* Father, Son, and Holy Ghost.
2. By their *Order of Subsistence:* the Father the first; the Son the second; and the Holy Ghost the third (but to mark their equality, they are sometimes mentioned in a different order).
3. By their different *Order of Operation:* the Father acts from himself through the Son and by the Spirit. The Son acts

from the Father and by the Spirit: And the Spirit acts from both the Father and the Son.

4. By their different *Stations* (which, in correspondence with their natural order of subsistence, they have voluntarily assumed in the work of our redemption): the Father as the Creditor, Judge Master, and Rewarder; the Son as the Mediator, Surety, and Servant; and the Holy Ghost as the Furnisher, Assistant, and Rewarder of the Mediator, and the Applier of the redemption purchased by him.[27]

I realize that this kind of theological study can seem cumbersome, but I wanted to highlight how the three expressions of God's nature never lose their individuality—even though they're inseparable. They're distinctive without being autonomous. They're revealed in both the "let us" and the "I am" passages. They never cease working towards the same purpose and goals, but they also never duplicate one another's efforts or step on each other's toes (although, I guess technically, they don't all have toes).

So when Jesus prays for his followers to become "one as he and the Father are one," he's not asking anyone to walk away from their individuality for the sake of unity. Rather, he calls his followers to learn how to move forward with one accord, *using the combined strengths of their individual attributes as a source of momentum*—not conflict. He calls us to "oneness," which isn't to be mistaken for "sameness."

Place Yourself

The way to triumph over the Assimilation Mutation Fury is through the spiritual anchor I call Place Yourself. It's the fourth of our five anchors. The goal of Placing Yourself is to meet the demands of the roles you've been given (breadwinner, homemaker, parent, spouse, friend, etc.), as well as the callings on your life (teacher, youth worker, pastor, evangelist, etc.), by taking full advantage of how God has uniquely equipped you.

Placing Yourself reconciles where you come from with where you are and (most importantly) where you're headed. It's a way of living so that the "you" God had in mind when he formed you in the womb is the "you" that ultimately comes forth—in all you do and all you are.

Placing Yourself guards against the theft of your identity as well as the surrender of your individuality. It's a tenet that helps you grow in confidence and contentment about who you really are. It also helps you safeguard the perfect design of one of God's most precious gifts to the world: *you*.

Let's look at a textbook example of the Place Yourself anchor in action, from the familiar story of David and Goliath. The background of the story has the nation of Israel at war with the neighboring Philistines. The two armies were encamped on either side of the Valley of Elah, but instead of engaging in full combat, they decided that each army would send out a single warrior to do one-on-one combat. The idea behind this was the belief that the stronger god would give their warrior the victory. This was a battle to establish both national and spiritual supremacy.

The Philistines sent out a seasoned warrior named Goliath. Goliath was a beast—and that's putting it mildly. He was about ten-feet tall, had coat of armor that weighed as much as an adult man, a spear with a bronze tip that weighed more than a bowling ball, and a specially forged sword that was unmatched anywhere in the world. The Israelites couldn't find anyone to fight Goliath—that is, not until David came along.

David was incensed by Goliath's arrogant threats, and volunteered to meet him on the battlefield. When Saul, the king of Israel heard about it, he had David brought into the king's chambers, which is where we pick up the narrative:

> Then Saul gave David his own armor—a bronze helmet and a coat of mail. David put it on, strapped the sword over it, and took a step or two to see what it was like, for he had never worn such things before. "I can't go in these," he protested to Saul. "I'm not used to them." So David took them off again. He picked up five smooth stones from a stream and put them into his shepherd's bag. Then, armed only with his shepherd's staff and sling, he started across the valley to fight the Philistine. As Goliath moved closer to attack, David quickly ran out to meet him. Reaching into his shepherd's bag and taking out a stone, he hurled it with his sling and hit the Philistine in the forehead. The stone sank in, and Goliath stumbled and fell face down on the ground. So David triumphed over the Philistine with only a sling and a stone. (1 Sam. 17: 38–40, 48–50, NLT)

When we study David's life, we see he has special gifts as both a musician and a warrior. These gifts help him succeed throughout his life. In the story, King Saul wants David to fight Goliath wearing the king's armor. No doubt, the king's armor was the finest to be had, and I'm sure King Saul not only wanted to provide the best military gear available for David, but also felt that David should have been honored by the offer. But if David had given in, it would have been a matter of fighting the right war with the wrong gifts. David refused the offer, trusting instead in his god-given instincts as a warrior and, as a result, achieved one of the greatest victories in history.

Like David, as we go through life we'll encounter people who will try to get us to fight the right fight the wrong way. They'll try to get us to use their gifts (or gifts they're familiar with) as we serve in the faith community. They mean well, but when we lay our gifts aside or use them in a manner other than how God has shown us, we betray who we really are. If we continue to operate like this, we start to lose sight of who we really are.

The Place Yourself anchor keeps us from ever reaching this point of confusion.

Place Yourself 101: What Is Man?

Oscar Wilde observed: "Most people are other people. Their thoughts are someone else's opinions, their lives a mimicry, their passions a quotation."

The pressure to be what others expect is alive and well in the faith community, but you don't have to surrender to it. Your mission is to learn how to contribute to the faith community without sacrificing who God has created you to be in the process. How do you bring your unique characteristics to the faith community without surrendering them to the faith community? For starters, it helps if you understand *whom* God has made you—*and why.*

The eighth psalm asked the question: "What are mere mortals that you should think about them, human beings that you should care for them? Yet you made them only a little lower than God and crowned them with glory and honor" (Ps 8:4–5, NLT).

In the book of Genesis, we learn that we're made in God's image and likeness. Through further study, we discover our nature includes a spirit, soul, and body

One of the more popular sayings among people of today's faith community is, "Man is not a physical being having a *spiritual* experience, but a spiritual being having a *physical* experience!" The statement is talking about the proper outlook that we (as people of faith) should have regarding our life on earth. It's a catchy quote, and an admirable sentiment. However, I can't completely agree with it.

I don't agree with the overall message, which suggests that the human spirit is the "legitimate" part of our nature, leaving the body and soul as runner-ups. Based on this kind of thinking, the human spirit primarily deals with "important" spiritual matters and eternity, while the body and soul merely handle the consolation prizes of temporary, earth-related stuff.

Once people get this idea in their heads, it's only a matter of time before they start minimizing the purpose and value of the body and the soul. In time, the body and soul will be neglected, belittled, and even vilified (this is a core belief in one school of Gnosticism).

While it's true that the human spirit is the part of our nature designed to interact with the Spirit of God, that doesn't mean it's more important than the other God-given, God-formed parts of our nature. God created human beings to live on, enjoy, and have dominion over the earth. The three parts of our nature are essential to fulfilling this purpose.

Without a body, we couldn't enjoy the magnificent smell of cherry blossoms in the fall, the hopeful sounds of children laughing on a playground, or the lip smacking taste of Mediterranean-grilled chicken.

Without a soul we couldn't study our galaxy's astronomical motion, feel the swell of love and pride as our child walks across the stage to receive his or her diploma, or decide between a noisy get together with friends or a quiet evening with a cup of hot cocoa and a good book (author's note: *pick the book*).

Without a Spirit, we couldn't sense a world beyond our five natural senses, have an inherent awareness of right and wrong, or have a reliable compass in our pursuit of godliness.

If you remove the spirit, you're simply left with a corpse. If you remove the soul, all you have is a vegetable. If you remove the body, then all you've got is a ghost. The physical body ages, wears out, and ultimately dies in time. Nevertheless, in the afterlife, a person gets an "incorruptible" body—another actual body, not just an apparition or a vaporous aura. So, whether a man or woman is in the present earthly realm or the realm of eternity, they'll always have all three parts intact—if not, then you're not dealing with a man or woman.

For Temperamental Reasons

While we know we each have a spirit, soul, and body, we also need to realize that they're not all made the same. Even after we're born again, converted, saved, baptized, and Spirit-filled, we still have deep issues about ourselves that we need to understand.

A major factor in determining who we are is something called temperament. In psychology, temperament refers to those aspects of an individual's personality (such as introversion or extroversion) that are often regarded as innate rather than learned.[28]

Temperament is native to each person and different from one person to the next. It largely accounts for our individual moods, emotions, likes, and behavior. Our general disposition and approach to life is connected to our temperament.

Hippocrates believed that an individual's temperament was largely determined by activity levels of the four humors (fluids) found in the body (blood, yellow bile, black bile, and phlegm). He believed that these bodily fluids caused mental and physiological changes that influenced brain activity and thus behavior. The physiological and mental aspects make temperament a matter of soul *and* body.

I view temperament as the *soil of the soul*. When you look at the different regions of our planet, you see different soil types in different regions. For example, Georgia is famous for its thick red clay, Illinois for its deep black topsoil, Egypt for its mineral-rich silt, and the Arabian Desert for its shifting sand. In the same way, each person has a unique composition to his or her "human soil."

Note that the soil in any region doesn't change. You can mix additives or treatments into the soil, which might allow you to grow things that the soil wouldn't normally support. But when all these additives are worn out or washed out, the soil reverts to its natural state.

The same can be said for human temperament. In certain environments, our behavior adjusts, but our underlying temperament doesn't change. Like the leopard, we really can't change our spots.

There are four basic temperaments, which can be combined to create sixteen blended temperament models. The concept of four basic temperaments also corresponds with the biblical reference to temperament found in Proverbs 30. Here's a description of each basic temperament, using Hippocrates' names:

Sanguine. The sanguine temperament is fundamentally impulsive and pleasure-seeking; sanguine people are sociable and emotional. They enjoy social gatherings, making new friend,s and can be boisterous. They're usually creative and often daydream. Sanguines can also be sensitive, compassionate, and thoughtful. Sanguine personalities generally struggle with following tasks all the way through, are chronically late, and tend to be forgetful and sometimes a little sarcastic.

Often, when they pursue a new hobby, they lose interest as soon as it ceases to be engaging or fun. They are "people" persons—talkative and not shy. Their core strengths include being ambitious, compassionate, and outgoing. Their core weaknesses include being prone to exaggeration, disorganized, and restless. President Ronald Reagan, Magic Johnson, and King David are well-known sanguines.

Choleric. The choleric temperament is fundamentally ambitious and leader-like. They have a lot of aggression, energy, and passion, and try to instill it in others. They can be stubborn and very direct. They can dominate people of other temperaments, especially phlegmatic types.

Many great charismatic military and political figures were choleric. They like to be in charge. Their core strengths include being strong-willed, independent, and goal-oriented. Their core weaknesses include being domineering, unforgiving, and unsympathetic. Alexander the Great, Bill Gates, and the Apostle Paul are well-known cholerics.

Melancholic. The melancholic temperament is fundamentally introverted and thoughtful. Melancholic people are often pondering and considerate, getting worried when they're late for events. Melancholics can be highly creative in activities such as poetry and art, and can become preoccupied with the tragedy and cruelty in the world.

Melancholics can be perfectionists, self-reliant, and independent. They can get so involved in what they're doing they forget to think of others. Their core strengths include being analytical, self-disciplined, and loyal. Their core weaknesses include being deeply emotional, easily offended, and suspicious. Charles Darwin, Hamlet, and the Prophet Elijah were all famous melancholics.

Phlegmatic. The phlegmatic temperament is fundamentally relaxed and quiet, ranging from warmly attentive to lazily sluggish. Phlegmatics tend to be content with themselves. They are accepting and affectionate. They may be receptive and shy and often prefer stability to uncertainty and change.

They're consistent, relaxed, calm, rational, curious, and observant. They can also be passive-aggressive. Their core strengths include being diplomatic, agreeable, and objective. Their core weaknesses include being unmotivated, indecisive, and subject to procrastination. President Calvin Coolidge, Tim Duncan, and Queen Esther are famous phlegmatics.[29]

Everyone has a primary and secondary temperament type (I happen to be a choleric/sanguine). It's important to know your personal temperament and understand the strengths and liabilities of your own "human soil." You'll be amazed at how accurate the temperament study models are.

In his book *Please Understand Me,* Dr. David Keirsay introduced a self-assessed personality questionnaire (the Keirsey Temperament Sorter) which helps to identify your temperament type. Additionally, Dr. Tim LaHaye has written several excellent books on the subject, including *The Spirit Controlled Temperament.* I suggest you take a look at some of their material or other material on the subject.

Why is this important? Because understanding your temperament gives you a basis for knowing your strengths and weaknesses, assets and liabilities. It helps to know, for instance, that you're naturally inclined to be talkative, suspicious, moody, agreeable, or strong-willed. Having insight into the root of some of your behaviors can be a big advantage.

Just a quick note: even though temperaments don't change, God's grace can sustain us and equip us to overcome any temperament-based setback. Without him , we could become victims of our own nature, but with him , we rise as victors instead.

Place Yourself 201: Place Markers

This above all: to thine own self be true,
And it must follow, as the night the day,
Thou canst not then be false to any man.[30]

This famous line from the play *Hamlet* is the kind of sound advice that all of us can benefit from. However, it can be confusing to a person who doesn't have a clear idea of the "own self" they're supposed to be true to.

The New Testament expands this idea, adding our relationship with God as the key factor to understanding and being true to ourselves:

> Cultivate your own relationship with God, but don't impose it on others. You're fortunate if your behavior and your belief are coherent. But if you're not sure, if you notice that you are acting in ways inconsistent with what you believe—some days trying to impose your opinions on others, other days just trying to please them—then you know that you're out of line. If the way you live isn't consistent with what you believe, then it's wrong. (Rom. 14:22–23 AMP).

Ultimately, only you and your creator can solve the mystery of who you're supposed to be; but I'd like to offer a few points of advice that should help. I call these points "Place Markers." They're tips and guidelines that help define and clarify your complete identity. They help you Place Yourself. Let's go right into them.

Place Marker #1: Bring Out the Nukes

One of my favorite passages is in the fourth chapter of the Gospel of Luke. Let's look at it briefly:

> [17] The scroll of Isaiah the prophet was handed to him. He unrolled the scroll and found the place where this was written:
> [18] "The Spirit of the LORD is upon me, for he has anointed me to bring Good News to the poor. He has sent me to proclaim that captives will be released, that the blind will see, that the oppressed will be set free,
> [19] and that the time of the LORD's favor has come."

²⁰ He rolled up the scroll, handed it back to the attendant,
and sat down. All eyes in the synagogue looked at him
intently.

²¹ Then he began to speak to them. "The Scripture you've
just heard has been fulfilled this very day!" (Lk 4:17–22, NLT)

There are two "place marker" lessons I'd like to draw from this passage. The first lesson comes from verse 17, where Jesus takes the
scroll and "turns to the place where it was written"—*about him.* Just
as there were specific scriptures in the Bible written about Jesus,
there are also specific scriptures in the Bible written *about you.*

I call these "Nuclear Passages," because they address the core
purposes (*nucleus*) for which you've been created, and they provide
an energy resource (*nuclear*) to fuel the fulfillment of that purpose.
They'll also blow away any attack against your authentic spiritual identity.

How do you find them? Great question. Here's my answer: you
don't find them—they come to you in the normal course of living (which
should include times of prayer, meditation, and scriptural study).

For example, one of my Nuclear Passages—Isaiah 50:4—simply
exploded in my spirit when I heard it quoted at a funeral. The
moment I heard it, something literally "dropped" into my innermost being. The sensation was like a large boulder dropped from a
helicopter into a deep lake. Internally, I felt the initial "ker-splunk"
as this passage plunged through the surface of my spirit, followed
by a sense of something very weighty sinking into the depths of my
being. I couldn't focus on anything else for the rest of the service.
Decades later, this passage is still a vibrant reminder of my purpose
and calling and a resource of inspiration to pursue that purpose.

The second lesson from this passage comes from verse 21. Jesus
raised every eyebrow in the synagogue when he boldly declared that

he was the fulfillment of the scripture he had just read. This brings me to my next place marker:

Place Marker #2: Say What God Says About You

In the previous passage, Jesus boldly declared that this promise was fulfilled, even though at the time he hadn't done any of the things mentioned in the passage. That's how faith works; it believes, declares, and proclaims before things have materialized.

Once you've "found yourself" in the Bible (especially your Nuclear Passages), be sure to speak those scriptures over your life constantly. Study them, say them aloud, and agree with them until they're firmly embedded in your spirit, soul, and body.

Do I believe in personal prophecy? Yes, especially in the sense of prophesying to *myself*. I make sure to pray, quote, declare, and conduct myself according to what God's Word says about me. You may not see a change overnight—in fact, you may not see any change over the course of several years. Nevertheless, make a practice of consistently agreeing with God's Word about you. In due time, the change *will* come.

Let me refer back to my "nuclear passage" from Isaiah 50:4 for a moment. When I first heard it, somehow I knew God wanted to use me as an encourager and an exhorter, but I had no idea what to say that could help people. When people would share their problems, I was as perplexed about what to do or say as they were. But, as I continued to declare this passage over my life, something amazing started happening.

First, God started giving me deeper insight into his Word as I studied it. Secondly, he started giving me insight into other people's situations. He allowed me to understand things from their perspectives, and to understand their pains, fears, and worries.

Finally, God taught me how he saw their circumstances, and he started giving me the words to say that would strengthen them or provide direction. Sometimes these words addressed their problems head-on. At other times, the words bolstered their faith in the face of their trials.

Once God gives you a "nuclear passage," write it down, read it often, speak it often, and make it a daily necessity.

Place Marker #3: Spend Time with People Who Value Your Call and Purpose

Jesus chose twelve disciples to be both students and assistants in his earthly ministry. In time, three of these twelve—Peter, James, and John—seemed to rise in prominence above the others.

Jesus selected these three to go with him into Jairus' house when he raised Jairus' daughter from the dead. The same three were picked to accompany him on Mt. Hermon, where he was transfigured. When Jesus wrestled in prayer in the Garden of Gethsemane, he asked Peter, James, and John to watch and pray with him .

It wasn't that Jesus liked these three men better than the others. Nor was it the case that they were better suited for ministry than the others. In fact, they were no greater than any of the other disciples, with this exception: they seemed to have a greater appreciation for Jesus' call and a greater desire to see his purpose fulfilled.

God will send people into your life who will realize your calling and purpose, and who'll value both. They'll be aware of your spiritual gifts and your strengths, and they will respect what God wants to do in your life. They're invaluable supporters, especially during the "ugly duckling" stages when what you are has little resemblance to what you'll eventually become.

Not only will they understand your calling and purpose, but they'll also value you as an individual—not just based on your spiritual gifts. You won't come across a lot of people like this, but when you do, be sure to thank God for them. They are rare treasures on the sea of life, sent by your Heavenly Father to encourage you and bolster your faith.

They may not have an impressive spiritual resumé, but they have the one thing that is essential in this kind of relationship: they love you and they see the purpose to which God has called you.

On a visit to the Palm Springs area, Oral Roberts made a comment that I will never forget. He said, "If you ever need help in your ministry and you have to choose between a candidate who has all the qualifications but doesn't seem to be gung ho about you and your ministry, and a candidate who loves you and the work you're doing but doesn't seem to have all the qualifications, *always pick the one who loves you.* God can give a person whatever skills they lack, but he won't make a person love you, and that can make all the difference in your success or failure."

Place Marker #4: Take the E-A-T Test

The first two-way conversation ever recorded between God and man begins awkwardly, with God asking Adam two questions that undoubtedly left Adam feeling uncomfortable. Good questions will do that sometimes, and these were both good questions.

At the risk of sounding obvious, I'd like to point to the fact that God never asks a question for lack of the answer. His questions are always asked for our benefit—not his. They challenge us to pause and reflect on whatever it is we're thinking, speaking, feeling, or doing and choose something better, something higher. These two questions, in particular, help us refocus our sights, recover our footing, and retrieve to our proper place. I call this the *Eden Aptitude Test* (*E-A-T* for short).

E-A-T Question #1: Where Are You?

The first question is "Where are you?" (Gen. 3:9). Three simple words. No innuendo or double-meaning. However, the question required Adam to make an honest assessment of where he stood in comparison to where he *should have been.*

If you've ever had to take a hard look at yourself when you've lost your way—when you've blown it—you know this kind of self-examination can be difficult. Like Adam, sometimes our reckless behavior and poor choices keep us so preoccupied that we lose sight of just how far out of place we become.

It's not by chance that "Where are you?" is the first question God *ever* asked. It demonstrates his fatherly concern for our well-being, in view of our inclination to get into trouble. But it's not a punitive question. It's not designed to put Adam on the spot, make him feel ashamed, or condemn him. On the contrary, it's a question that brims with redemptive purpose and hope—a lifeline to a child flailing in deep water over his head. It's a question meant to help him stop before things get worse, regain his footing, and return to his rightful place.

I like the version of this question that I hear my kids using. It's worded differently but it carries the same message: *"Check yourself before you wreck yourself."*

Throughout the day, it's fitting to ask yourself "Where are you?" Where are you in relation to the Nuclear Passages in your life? Where are you in comparison to the vision God has placed in your heart and the roles he's called you to fill?

Don't beat yourself up with this question. If you find that you've gotten off track, prayerfully make the adjustments to recover your place. If it seems like you're on track but stalled, don't panic. Remain faithful and develop patience. The things you believe in lie on the path ahead. As you persist, you'll come to them.

If you keep having some of the same problems over and over, but you're having a hard time seeing any fault in your own behavior (i.e., you're usually an innocent "victim" of your circumstances or other people's bad choices), I suggest you add the following prayer to your times of self-examination: "Point out anything in me that offends you, and lead me along the path of everlasting life" (Ps 139:24, NLT).

E-A-T Question #2: Who Told You You Were Naked?

The second question, "Who told you you were naked?" goes right to the heart of one of the enemy's most effective weapons against us—sowing the seeds of doubt. This has to do with thoughts and words that unsettle us concerning what we're about, what we're doing, and what God wants for us.

"Who told you you were naked?" is a question that can apply to other issues like: "Who told you you were unqualified?"; "Who told you you were too young—or too old?"; "Who told you you needed a college degree?"; or any number of qualifications that we seem to lack.

It's critical to remember one thing about this question—and if you can keep this in mind you should pass this test every time. Adam had always been naked, and up until then his nakedness hadn't been a problem for him or God. God's not banking on your ability. Whatever he wants you to do, he'll equip you to do it, regardless of what anyone else thinks. Your *availability* is much more important than your ability. He needs you available physically, mentally, and spiritually.

The first word of this question (Who) points to an outsider's role in bringing confusion to Adam's understanding of himself. This is usually the case. In the Garden of Eden, the outsider is Satan, and his motives were intentional—he wanted to confuse man.

For those familiar with sports, this is the spiritual equivalent of "trash talk." It's strictly designed to get you off your game . . . to distract you because someone doesn't want you to reach your potential.

The "who" could be an adversary, but in some cases it will be someone who cares for you but just doesn't understand God's purpose and calling for your life. The "who" could be a parent, a sibling, a friend, a teacher, or even a pastor. They'll often give you advice based on their assessment of what's safest (versus risky) for you.

Jesus faced the same issues throughout his earthly ministry, whether it was his mother and siblings thinking he was out of his mind (see Mk. 3:21) or one of his disciples telling him that his talk of laying down his life was the ramblings of foolishness (see Mk. 8:31–33).

No matter how well-meaning people may be, you must learn to identify the harmful seeds of doubt. People will often want you to fit into a certain position or carry out a duty in a way that goes against your inner spiritual compass. They may question you, press you, or otherwise compel you to conform to what they have in mind.

When this happens, take the person aside and explain how you feel about the situation. Try to be prepared to offer a couple of alternative solutions that still take care of this matter *without* violating your sense of who God has called you to be. In either case, whether the influence comes from the devil or people, I like to counteract the "who" in the second question with the following "who" question: "If God be for me *who* can be against me?" (Rom. 8:21).

In the end, recognize and isolate the source of doubt, learn to stand up, and stand firm on the vision God has given you for you.

Place Marker #5: Pay Attention to Your P's

There are four words in particular—all that begin with the letter "p"—that represent a familiar pattern that God often uses to bring about his will in your life. The words are *problem, promise, person, and place.*

The *problem* identifies what's lacking, painful, or wrong in a situation. The *promise* is God's spoken or written word regarding that *problem*. The *person* is the human who is sensitive to the *problem*, aware of the *promise*, and positioned to respond in faith. Lastly, the *place* is the physical or spiritual portal where faith is released and the problem is resolved. I'd like to point out a few facts about the *place*.

Places are significant in the course of our lives—*and* in God's grand scheme. Certain events *only* happen at a designated place. Sometimes this designated place is a physical location.

For example, the Running of the Bulls event during the San Fermin festival takes place *in* Pamplona, Spain. Or consider that Jesus Christ had to be born *in* Bethlehem, in accordance with ancient prophecy. If you wanted to attend either of these events, you'd have to be in one of those places.

At other times, however, the designated place isn't a physical location, but rather a *setting* created through our faith, worship, and obedience. For example, the scriptures promise that the presence of the Lord would come wherever two or three believers gather in his name.

Similarly, God's presence inhabits sincere praise—whether offered by a group or an individual. Whether a physical location or a spiritual setting, every encounter with God—and the release of his power in the earth on our behalf—is always connected to the right *place*.

With that in mind, whenever we set out to receive something from God or achieve something with God, we should always check to make sure we're in the right place, keeping in mind the fact that God retains the option to *change* the place.

Like the Israelites who followed the pillar of fire by night and the pillar of cloud by day, we have to develop a close enough relationship with God to be aware of his movement, so we can move as he moves. Portals are opened and realities are exchanged when we find the right *place*.

Place Marker #6: Staring Down Intimidation

If people in your faith circles are compelling you to do things you're uncomfortable with, it's probably time to confront them and discuss it. Confronting people who are causing difficulties in your life—even those who mean well—is a major challenge for most people. Even when there's little possibility of an angry reaction or retaliation, some people still avoid confrontation at all costs.

However, your satisfaction with life often increases or decreases with your willingness to confront people who play a role in trying to box you in. The real problem is intimidation, and the root of the intimidation is *fear*.

In his book, *Breaking Intimidation*, John Bevere says, "Since intimidation is a spirit, it cannot be fought on the level of our intellect or will. Having a positive mental attitude will not overcome intimidation. Spiritual resistance requires spiritual assistance."[31]

I suggest that you pull out a piece of paper and write down a detailed list of the things that you're afraid of, intimidated by, and uncomfortable with (related to your church or group). Next, rank each item on the list from one to five (one being least bothered by, five being most bothered by).

Spend some time praying about the items on the list; include scriptures that deal with the fear and intimidation in your praying (a few to start with are 2 Tim. 2:1, 1 Cor. 16:13, and Joshua 1:7). Call the person that you need to confront and schedule a time when you can either meet or speak over the phone about the situation. Go through the list item by item (when possible, be sure to suggest alternate ways of doing things). I provide some additional strategies for dealing with fear and intimidation in the chapter on Waste Yourself.

Place Marker #7: Micah's Memo

The final "place marker" also happens to be another of my personal "nuclear passages." It's found in the book of Micah: "He has showed you, O man, what is good. And what does the Lord require of you? To act justly and to love mercy and to walk humbly with your God" (Mic. 6:8 NLT).

This passage reminds us of three foundational footings that not only help hold us in place, but also support the weight of what God wants to bring about in our lives. The three footings are *acting justly*, *loving mercy*, and *walking humbly with your God*.

The first footing, *acting justly*, is a matter of conduct that flows out of two guiding principles: a) considering what God expects of us, based on what we've learned from the scriptures, and b) making sure our conduct doesn't violate our moral compass.

Essentially, *acting justly* is a call for us to consistently do what's right and good as we understand it. We resist the appeal of relativism and live by the rock-solid principles of godliness—without exceptions. The epistle to the believers in Rome sums this up: "Blessed is the one who has no reason to pass judgment on himself for what he approves. For whatever does not proceed from faith is sin" (Rom. 14:22b, 23b ESV).[32]

The second footing is to *love mercy*, which is a call to always extend forgiveness and compassion to people—*including ourselves*. Consider the following excerpt on mercy, taken from *The Merchant of Venice*:

> The quality of mercy is not strained.
> It drops as the gentle rain from heaven
> Upon the place beneath. It is twice blest:
> It blesses him that gives and him that takes.[33]

In the courts of reconciliation, mercy outranks judgment and puts supernatural healing, forgiveness and restoration within everyone's reach.

Humility before God is the final footing in this passage. Humility before God is an attitude of meekness, modesty, and honoring God's sovereignty in our lives. It's a willingness to endure injustice, dishonor, and misunderstanding because we trust God's ability to superintend the affairs of our life. Humility before God is the cornerstone of greatness in God's sight.

Humility *before God* is different from the type of personal humility we see commonly *within ourselves.* Personal humility shows respect for one's self and others, but rarely moves beyond that. Humility before God also differs from embarrassment (which is really a flare-up of pride).

As we mature and grow in the faith, we're able to consistently conduct ourselves according to Micah's compelling message. This consistency provides a tremendous anchor to our lives—one that holds us in place even through the toughest times.

Place Yourself 301: Somebody up There Likes You

Your individuality is one of God's greatest and most precious gifts. He's made each of us so unique that in his sight even identical twins are as different as a catfish from a maple tree.

Jesus gives us a glimpse further into the degree that God takes each of us into account when he shares the fact that even the very hairs of your head are all numbered (Lk. 12:7). This isn't talking about God knowing the total follicle-count for each of our heads (which he does), but rather it means that each hair on our head has a separate, distinct ID number—and God knows each of those numbers for each of us.

God knows when hair #2,645 comes out when you shower, when hair #1,021 is pulled out while brushing, or when hair #478 is left on the pillow.

Unfortunately, the Assimilation Mutation Fury emphasizes "sameness" as an "easier" way to create unity. But whatever is gained through this "sameness" approach pales in comparison to what's lost in the process.

What's lost, many times, is the individual traits, attributes, and qualities we each bring to the community of faith—the same traits we've been given to add fullness and zing to the thinned out patches of life. What gets lost is our distinctive creative seasoning that helps keeps life appetizing.

When everyone is compelled to be the same, we lose the one-of-a-kind moments like Barbara Streisand accepting an unspoken dare to reach for a vibrato note in an octave somewhere near Ursa Major, or Michael Jordan electrifying a crowd by dunking from the foul line with his tongue sticking out.

This sameness approach doesn't support people who don't follow the conventional paths of uniformity. It frowns on people like the lanky backwoods anthropology student with virtually no formal theological training who thinks he can be a preacher (Billy Graham), or the shy teen who can't read a note of music or even hold a conversation without stuttering badly, yet wants to write and perform songs about God's love all over the world (Andraé Crouch).

God created you the way he did for a reason. He takes pride in how he's formed you and in the gifts he's placed within you. He's blessed when we use those gifts appreciatively and thankfully.

When sameness is the order of the day, the *you* God had in mind when he formed you in your mother's womb gets covered up. The Assimilation Mutation Fury makes sure that "you" disappear over time, which is why in a sea of distinctively created people it's often hard to spot an original.

Love-In-Action: A Placement Test

Like most of the lessons in this book, the Place Yourself principle wasn't something that just dropped into my lap or that I learned through osmosis. I saw it modeled in the lives of godly men and women, but God saw to it that the appropriate hardships and trials made their way into my life so that I could learn *to Place Myself firsthand*. I'd like to share an experience in which the Place Yourself principle became a turning point in my life.

When I was in my early twenties, I founded a non-profit organization called Love-in-Action. The purpose of the group was to provide spiritual fellowship services for senior citizen communities.

I got the idea because, at the time, I was working a job that required me to service a number of senior citizen homes. From conversations with these elderly tenants, I found out many of them were no longer able to fellowship with other Christians outside of the senior home, mostly due to health problems or lack of transportation.

Some had spent their entire lives serving and working in the faith community, but now they were isolated and, in some cases, completely abandoned. I thought this was tragic and decided to do something about it.

Love-in-Action was, basically, a Christian singing group consisting of several gifted young people ranging in age from sixteen to twenty-two. Since the people at the senior homes were from different Christian backgrounds, I thought it best to have an ecumenical approach to this ministry. We weren't going to push any specific denominational agenda. We wanted to be as broad-based as possible in order to be a blessing to as many people as we could. I came up with a general format for our "services" that met all these objectives.

I talked it over with my pastor (my dad) and received his permission and blessing to move forward with the project. He also gave me some great advice on organizational details. We held our first event about a month later, and were off and running. That's when things really got interesting.

My dad was both a pastor and a regional official in his church organization. When some of the officials above him heard about what I was doing, they wanted Love-in-Action to be associated with their denomination. Additionally, they felt I needed to become an ordained minister, due to the faith-based nature of the work I was doing.

Well, I wasn't going to attach their name to our organization because I felt it would work against the ecumenical reputation we'd already established. As far as becoming an ordained minister, that was the furthest thing from my mind. I just couldn't see how being ordained had any bearing on what I was already doing.

But the "label crew" was very persistent. They insisted, "You're doing the work of a minister, so you need ministerial credentials. Furthermore, this kind of organization needs the proper legal covering and accountability." Eventually I said okay to ordination. Our denomination had specific programs for ordination, but I fast-tracked it and was ordained within a year. However, I stood my ground about Love-in-Action remaining independent from any particular church or denominational affiliation.

There were other pressures from the faith community regarding this outreach. As I mentioned earlier, we were essentially a singing group—and a pretty good singing group at that. By this time in my life, I already had a few studio albums under my belt, so we had very good musicians working with us. We also had a group of fantastic singers.

Once the word got out about our group, we were bombarded with invitations to sing at local churches, musicals, concerts, or other events. I declined all of these invitations because that's not what the group was created to do.

Our initial focus remained on the senior citizen communities. Later we expanded the focus to include other interned groups—like mental health and rehabilitation centers. But I didn't see our role as performing in church or similar public venues . . . we wanted to reach out to the left outs.

I felt that there were plenty of singing groups already available for church concerts, youth events, etc. Well, that didn't go over too well with my brothers and sisters within the faith community. We were accused of being sectarian, haughty, unsupportive, and having a hidden agenda. But that was just the start.

As I mentioned earlier, I had become an ordained minister. The majority of pastors and ministers in this particular denomination were powerful preachers and skilled orators. They brought a lot of energy, charisma, and enthusiasm to the pulpit. They worked up the crowds. Some of these guys were so talented they could preach the red paint right off a stop sign. I was nothing like that. As Charles Swindoll put it, "Do you ever get the idea that life is a violin solo and you're wearing mittens?" That was me among this group.

I was just as sincere and committed to the cause of Christ as anyone else, but I was more comfortable speaking to a congregation in my usual voice and tone. I spoke with solid conviction; I just wasn't comfortable sounding like a cross between a ring announcer and an auctioneer. I was respected within our church community for my skills as a musician, but when it came to my ability as a minister, I probably left many people scratching their heads.

On several occasions, I got "pep talks" from other ministers who advised me to "give the people what they expected and were used to." "Just let go and let God." I tried it for a while, and as a result, I noticed that I was getting more invitations to speak at different churches. But it just didn't fit me—like David trying to wear Saul's armor. At times, I felt like I was performing.

Ultimately, I ignored the pressure to be like other preachers within that faith circle and stuck with what was true to my nature. I admired the oratorical skills of these preachers, and have nothing against that style of preaching—in fact, I actually enjoy it. It just wasn't for me. I didn't realize it at the time, but if I had adopted that particular preaching style, I would have narrowed the field of people I'd be able to reach effectively.

Remember, life is a journey . . . a personal journey. It's your journey and your story, so don't live it based on someone else's narrative. When you reach your destination, you want to make sure that you arrive with your purpose intact (and if possible, all your own teeth).

It takes time to understand and grow into the person God has created you to be. It can't happen without your consent, cooperation, and perseverance. In the end, it's worth the investment.

Epilogue

It's probably natural to think about how the information in this chapter could help others, especially if you have people in mind who you think would really benefit from it. Before you do that, however, first make sure that you apply the teaching in this chapter to your own life. This anchor admonishes you to Place *Yourself*—not your spouse, your child, a relative, friend, or associate.

Focus on learning, growing, and implementing this teaching in *your own* life. Please don't lose sight of the fact that this book is written for your benefit *first*.

Fred Rogers was a Presbyterian minister, educator, musician, and television host best known for his *Mister Rogers' Neighborhood* program on PBS. He often used music to teach life lessons to his audience. One of his simplest tunes carries the powerful lyrics that captured God's love of the unique design and essence of each person—a uniqueness that we should all come to appreciate in ourselves and in others.

The song has been recorded and performed by multiple artists (my personal favorite is Amy Grant's version from the "Songs from the Neighborhood" project). The lyrics remain as powerful and liberating today as when he first wrote them in the early 70s:

> It's you I like,
> It's not the things you wear,
> It's not the way you do your hair--
> But it's you I like
> The way you are right now,
> The way down deep inside you--
> Not the things that hide you,
> Not your toys--
> They're just beside you.
>
> But it's you I like--
> Every part of you,
> Your skin, your eyes, your feelings
> Whether old or new.
> I hope that you'll remember
> Even when you're feeling blue
> That it's you I like,
> It's you yourself,
> It's you, it's you I like.[34]
> Place Yourself.

Chapter 8

GRACE
YOURSELF

Understanding spiritual growth

If you've ever done a belly-flop off the high diving board you know it can be both an exhilarating and painful experience. The same can be said for bringing up the topic of "spiritual maturity" among a group of believers. This subject always seems to be accompanied by controversy and debate, even when discussed among people within the same circles. Exactly what is it? How is it achieved? Who evaluates it? What is its purpose? How will someone know when they've attained it? What's the benefit in pursuing it?

Look at the fascinating results from this 2009 survey, which asked two different focus groups the same question: How do you define spiritual maturity?

Group #1: Non-Pastors/Non-Spiritual Leaders
1. Having a relationship with Jesus   (21 percent)
2. Following rules and being obedient   (15 percent)
3. Living a moral lifestyle   (14 percent)
4. Possessing concern about others   (13 percent)

5. Being involved in spiritual disciplines   (13 percent)
6. Applying the Bible to life   (12 percent)
7. Being spiritual or having belief   (8 percent)
8. Sharing their faith with others   (6 percent)
9. Involvement in church activities   (5 percent)

Group #2: Pastors/Spiritual Leaders:
1. Practicing spiritual disciplines   (19 percent)
2. Involvement in church activities   (15 percent)
3. Sharing their faith to others   (15 percent)
4. Having a relationship with Jesus   (14 percent)
5. Having concern for others   (14 percent)
6. Applying the Bible to life   (12 percent)
7. Being willing to grow spiritually   (12 percent)
8. Having knowledge of Scripture   (9 percent)[35]

If nothing else, this study shows how much difference of opinion exists about what it is! It should be no surprise, then, that there's just as much variety of opinion on how it's achieved.

The pursuit of spiritual maturity has given rise to a range of dogmatic practices within the faith community. Some of these practices can be traced back to early church traditions—like fasting or foot-washing. The closest link others have seem to be old Twilight Zone episodes.

Snake-handlers, for example, who apparently view Mark 16:11 as more of a fraternity pledging ritual than a promise of divine protection. Holy men who sequester themselves behind fortified walls in order to limit their contact with an unfortified world that they're supposed to be fortifying. Polarized Protestants: in one corner a group who believes material wealth to be a reflection of one's spiritual maturity; in the other corner a group who believes that living two rungs beneath the poverty level is the real sign of spiritual maturity.

In all of this, one thing is clear: within the faith community, the subject of spiritual maturity breeds just as much confusion as consensus. Still, we have a scriptural mandate to grow—to move beyond where we are today. While the pathway to spiritual growth isn't always clear, it's still a mandate that can't be overlooked—especially now.

Breathe In . . .

Spiritual development isn't a *natural* process, but it is a *necessary* process. It's a necessary process because the faith community isn't an institution—it's an organism. The faith community is a contiguous living system.

The New Testament calls the community of faith "a building beyond nature, constructed of living stones" (1 Pet. 2:5). At the core, this "building" is *relational*, not *religious*. These relationships extend vertically (towards God) and horizontally (towards people).

When healthy, these relationships don't just lie like a dry stick on the sidewalk—they continue to grow vibrantly. This is significant, because all healthy organisms *must* grow. More importantly, growth is connected to spiritual maturity.

In order to evaluate "spiritual maturity," there has to be some standard of measurement—a scale or a checklist. We need a litmus test . . . right? It seems reasonable to use the Bible as our gauge. There's only one problem—that's *not* why it was written.

The Bible was never meant to be a scale. Unfortunately, it's misused this way all the time. This is one of the greatest ironies of the greatest book ever written.

John, the apostle, tells us exactly why the bible was written: "But these are written that you may believe…and that by *believing* you may have *life*" (Jn. 20:31 NLT).

Life. That's the central theme in the Bible. There's an unbreakable bond between belief and an upward spiraling life. Jesus reaffirmed this when he said: "I came that they may have and enjoy life, and have it in abundance (to the full, till it overflows)" (Jn. 10:10 AMP).

The Bible was given as a guide—a roadmap for the human quest of abundant life. This quest should culminate in the best life possible, in the here and now as well as the beyond. When our quests result in anything less, then something has gone wrong. Looking at the disjointed, distressed and distracted state of today's faith community, it's clear that something *has* gone wrong—horribly wrong.

Every time a congregation splits, it's a sign that something has gone wrong. When the majority of messages from the faith community leave people feeling burdened instead of lifted, it's a sign that something has gone wrong. When the faith community's focus and strongest influence is itself, it's a sign that something *is* wrong.

To understand what's wrong, we need look no further than the words written by one of history's greatest spiritual leaders, Paul the apostle: "The plan (of salvation) wasn't written out with ink on paper, with pages and pages of legal footnotes, killing your spirit. It's written with Spirit on spirit, his life on our lives!" (2 Co 3:6 MSG).

Paul makes it clear that the goal of experiencing abundant life isn't reached by using the Bible as a legal document. In fact, he says that's a recipe for spiritual disaster. Using the Bible as a *legal* document instead of a *living* document undermines its purpose. The Bible was written to give life, but this kind of scriptural wrangling suffocates life instead.

Compare this to the legal meaning of a marriage license. The license represents a union between two people—a union recognized by government and society. The married couple has all the rights that come with a legal marriage. However, if there's poor communication . . . no understanding . . . no compassion . . . no caring . . . and no love shared between that couple, then *who cares what that marriage license represents?*

They may be *legally* married, but their relationship can be a legal, living hell! Focusing on the legalities of such a marriage will never help their situation improve; in fact, it will probably make them feel more imprisoned in their circumstances.

There's a parallel to this condition within the faith community that I call *religiouslation.* Religiouslation defines and sanctions spiritual maturity by measuring one's behavior against a set of concepts extracted from the Bible. Religiouslation comes from un-matching bookends of "Thou Shalts" and "Thou Shalt Nots." These are contrived by the overzealous efforts of people who presume that God needs an editor. It's a system whose goal is to enforce strict adherence to its interpretations of approved spiritual behavior. Thou shalt believe *this way*—or else!

Religiouslation is polarizing and divisive. Believers use religiouslation in its different forms to justify cruelty, unkindness, and mercilessness towards others who see things differently.

Religiouslation is the faith community's kryptonite, wolf's bane, monkshood, and pride fall, all rolled up in one. As Paul indicated in the earlier passage, it will ultimately kill the very relationships that it claims it's designed to preserve.

Religiouslation isn't to be confused with the general term "religion." Religion is the service and worship of God or an observance of religious faith and beliefs. It's a term that covers man's attempt to include spirituality in his planet-bound understanding of things. Generally speaking, religion plays a positive role both to the individual and to society. However, religiouslation does not.

Madame de Staël was talking about religiouslation when she said that "religious life is not a peaceful hymn—it's a dreadful struggle."

It's also at the root of the harmful spiritual condition I call the *Are We There Yet?* Fury.

This Fury looks through a pseudo-spiritual lens constructed from these contrived interpretations and creates its own image of a "spiritually mature" person. It constantly measures a person's spiritual condition and progress against its own self-derived, self-serving standards.

If you measure up, you get the badge of approval. If you don't measure up, you're given the badge of condemnation (depending on the specific religious group, the consequences of not measuring up can get ugly fast). What most people aren't aware of is that the "badge of approval" is cut from the fabric of human pride and stitched with the threads of delusion.

Religiouslation gives a list of spiritual concepts to be measured against and a timeline for meeting these concepts. Failure to comply is a reason to bring into question one's spiritual condition. *"Are you really even saved in the first place?" "Others have conformed to these standards, what's wrong with you?"*

Religiouslation claims to be redemptive for humankind's sinful condition. The Bible teaches that there is only one redeemer—one mediator between God and man—Jesus Christ. Religiouslation says, "Nope, if you really want to get to know God you have to come through *us*!" Religiouslation implies that it is synonymous with God. It puts itself on a pedestal to be revered and esteemed—something reserved for God alone.

To really understand how maddening religiouslation can be, compare it to a person running a hundred-meter race. The runner crosses the finish line with a sense of satisfaction, but is shocked to see that the "officials" have suddenly decided to add another fifty meters to the race! So he runs the additional fifty meters, only to see that the finish line has been extended by another fifty meters. This continues endlessly, and that's exactly how religiouslation works. The focus isn't on finishing the race, it's on keeping you distractingly busy until all of your spiritual energy is exhausted.

Those suffering from the Are We There Yet? Fury have fallen prey to the influence of some form of religiouslation. They want to achieve spiritual maturity, which is good, but as country music artist Johnny Lee put it, they're "looking for love in all the wrong places."

Like a soggy, soured onion that stinks up the entire pantry, their shortcomings and failures are unpleasant reminders that they're not measuring up. Even more tragic, they wake up one day and realize that their joy, hope, and motivation for serving God is unexpectedly absent. It's all leaked out.

Have you ever felt like that? Are you in that boat now? Most of us who seek to achieve spiritual maturity have good motives. Foremost, we want to please God. We want our lives to be an effective witness to others, and we want to be fulfilled in our walk of faith.

However, when we try to accomplish these ends through the channels of religiouslation, we usually experience more condemnation than affirmation. We're usually more aware of our individual failures than our successes. We can't understand why our spiritual lives seem such an unfulfilling struggle.

Gradually, a sense of discouragement settles into our souls. One layer of "falling short" settles on top of another until we're trapped beneath an avalanche of unhealthy feelings tied to our woeful spiritual progress.

Eventually, many of us simply settle into spiritual dysfunction, and resign ourselves to, as Thoreau put it, "lead lives of quiet desperation and go to the grave with the song still in them." We give up, give in, and finally cave in.

So what's the answer? Glad you asked.

. . . Breathe Out

To begin with, the term "spiritual maturity" is a misnomer that tends to point people in the wrong direction (as far as achieving a healthy, growing relationship with God). Relationships aren't gratifying solely based on the level of *maturity* of the people involved.

Grade-schoolers, for example, can have gratifying relationships built around pulling hair, sticking a tongue out, or giving each other noogies. The *attention* and *regard* the two kids show each other is the reason the relationship is fulfilling—even though their silly actions seem to indicate the exact opposite. Still, these "childish" expressions are appropriate for them.

Let's not overlook the fact that the term *spiritual maturity* implies the existence of an ugly stepsister called *spiritual immaturity*. No one wants to be looked upon as spiritually immature. It's an unrewarding position to be shunned. In fact, most people see these two expressions as opposite ends on the spectrum of godly living. But is that perception accurate? No—not by a long shot.

Spiritual maturity and spiritual immaturity seem to be at odds with each other, but they're simply two components of one transaction—the amazing process of *spiritual growth*.

Ready, Set, Grow!

Let's move our focus away from spiritual maturity, and redirect it towards the process of spiritual growth. The process of spiritual growth is a study in *how* God works in believers' lives to transform them into the design he has for them. It's a study of movement—from glory to glory, from faith to faith.

Spiritual growth has much more to do with internal evolution than external alteration. It is godly change; from one thing to another thing, from one stage to the next, from one level to a different level.

A simple example of this is seen when a person first embraces the life of faith. They move *from* a state of separation from God to a state of union *with* God. They move from spiritual vagueness to spiritual preciseness—from spiritual unawareness to spiritual consciousness.

Each stage or season of spiritual growth is a specific experience involving a specific process. Specific transition points within these stages account for our movement.

All together, there are four primary stages of spiritual growth. Let's take a moment to examine each one.

Spiritual Growth Stage #1—Birthing

The *Birthing Stage* is the first phase of every spiritual growth process. During this stage, the dormant, core purposes for which you've been created are germinated and awakened to life. God's unmistakable fingerprints can be clearly seen at this stage—if you know where to look for them.

The Birthing Stage happens on God's schedule, not ours. It's not something we contrive or induce. As a rule, it comes without a hint, forethought, or clue. For example, one day you're satisfied as a homemaker, the next day you're consumed with a passion to help unwed teen mothers! One day you're happy driving a school bus with a settled work routine, the next day you're overwhelmed by the desire to feed the hungry.

Classic examples of the Birthing Stage from the scriptures include King David; an unsuspecting young shepherd suddenly called to be king (see 1 Sam. 16), Gideon; a man hiding in a barn, suddenly called to be the general of an elite army (see Judg. 6:11–8:21), and Peter; a rough-edged fisherman who was abruptly called from his boat to become one of Christianity's greatest leaders (see Matt. 4:18–20).

Spiritual Growth Stage #2—Hunger

The second stage of spiritual growth is the *Hunger Stage.* This is the stage when we seem to become living sponges. We consume everything we can that relates to whatever God has recently birthed in our lives. Our appetite for the things of God is voracious and insatiable.

We study, pray, fast—we give every spare moment to seeking knowledge about the new passion that burns in our souls. We often drive those closest to us nuts. We learn, learn . . . and then learn some more.

King David describes this Hunger Stage by saying: "I opened my mouth and panted with eager desire, for I longed for Your commandments" (Ps. 119:131 AMP).

Hundreds of years later, one of the New Testament authors added: "Like newborn babies, you must crave pure spiritual milk so that you will *grow* into a full experience of salvation. Cry out for this nourishment" (1 Pet. 2:2 NLT).

Just as a strong appetite is natural for a baby (and one of the signs of good health), a strong appetite for spiritual things is featured at this stage.

Spiritual Growth Stage #3—Rest

The third stage of spiritual growth is the *Rest Stage.* You expend a huge amount of energy during the Hunger Stage. Afterwards, not only are you full, but the high level of focus and consumption you maintained during the Hunger Stage will leave you exhausted— physically, mentally, and emotionally. Now, the cool-down period starts. It's time to rest—not just because you're tired, but so that your soul can properly absorb and digest all that you've taken in.

Our spiritual digestive system mirrors our natural digestive system. It matters not how much we take in, but rather how much we can actually digest and convert into useful energy. The Rest Stage is a crucial part of the soul's digestive process.

Luke is my favorite of the Gospels because it gives so much insight into Jesus' life during these critical "down-time" periods. Hans Margolius said, "Only in quiet waters things mirror themselves undistorted. Only in a quiet mind is adequate perception of the world."

This Rest Stage includes reduced personal activity, reduced involvement in non-essential affairs, prayer, meditation, quiet, reflection, self-examination, journaling, and sleep—among other things. New truths are incorporated into your character as you settle into an expanded form of being.

Spiritual Growth Stage #4—Reproduction

The fourth and final growth stage is the *Reproduction Stage*. It's at this point that we're able to reproduce—to perform—whatever God intended when he birthed this particular growth process. The Reproduction Stage follows the Rest Stage.

The Bible offers several clear examples of this sequence. For instance, after Jesus had spent forty days in the wilderness fasting and praying (Rest Stage), he immediately launched into an earthly ministry marked with inspired teaching, signs, and wonders (Reproduction Stage).

Or take, for instance, Moses, who after spending time exiled in a desert (Rest Stage), confronted the powers of Egypt that were responsible for his nation's captivity (Reproduction Stage). In each case the Rest Stage equipped and prepared them to fulfill God's purposes for their lives.

Everything that we've experienced throughout this particular spiritual process culminates at this stage. At the Reproduction Stage, we're ready to withstand adversity, overcome any challenges that face us, and impact our generation for God. We realize our calling and willingly take our place in serving. We can clearly see the outline of the road ahead and we're ready to advance. At this stage, the personal transformation needed to proceed with God's plan for us is complete.

These four stages of spiritual growth always occur sequentially and, as a whole, they make up an individual *spiritual growth process*. Each new Birthing Stage is an introduction to a specific spiritual growth process or spiritual growth experience. This spiritual growth process is, essentially, a specific personal learning journey. It's common to have several different spiritual growth processes taking place all at once.

For example, you can undergo a growth process that's developing your patience, while simultaneously a separate process can be underway to develop a musical gift you have. At the same time, you can be involved in a separate process to help you overcome some emotional wounds—perhaps freeing you from bitterness or insecurity.

The success of these growth processes hinges on our ability to work with the remarkable spiritual force called *grace*. Grace fortifies our lives at each stage of spiritual growth, providing the power needed to satisfy the demands of a particular spiritual growth experience. Grace also presides over the spiritual growth transition points that enable us to move forward.

Sometimes we'll move through these growth processes very quickly, while other times it will take us years and even decades—it all depends on how we receive and yield to the working of grace. No matter how difficult or easy the task before us, grace does the "heavy lifting" for us at each stage.

Godness Gracious

Conversion. Getting Saved. Accepting Christ. Coming to God. Salvation. You've probably heard one of these terms used to describe the primary birthing point of the spiritual growth experience. It's the initial event in which a person enters into a new phase of life, based on the choice to pursue a more authentic relationship with God.

I like to refer to this starting-point as being "born again," because (in spite of how this phrase has been distorted in contemporary society) it's the exact term that Jesus himself used when explaining this first step of transformed living. During a conversation one evening with a political leader named Nicodemus, Jesus turned to him and very matter-of-factly told him that in order to enter into this new phase of living "You *must* be *born again*" (Jn. 3:1–20).

This renewed life moves from a hopeful possibility to an unmistakable reality when a person wholeheartedly places his or her faith in God (a fitting response to the standing offer of faith God has already placed in them).

The scriptures are very clear about the fact that God initiated this relationship long ago—not man. Passages such as Romans 5:8 ("But God showed his great love for us by sending Christ to die for us while we were still sinners") and John 15:16 ("You didn't choose me, but I chose you"), show how God took the first steps to establish the relationship—long before we even had a clue that such a relationship was needed or even possible.

Teresa of Ávila said, "The feeling remains that God is on a journey, too." God's "journey" culminated in this remarkable demonstration of love towards humankind, which can best be described by one word: *grace*.

What is "grace" or, more specifically, what is "God's grace?" Within the faith community, the most popular definition of grace is "God's unmerited favor." I don't particularly care for this definition for three reasons.

First, any and every good thing we receive from God is *unmerited*. There's no expression of his love that can be merited (earned or purchased)—and grace is no exception.

Saying that grace is God's unmerited favor is like saying, "I'm going to pour a glass of wet water." Wetness is an intrinsic and unmerited feature of water—*all* water is wet. There's never been an instance of *dry* water and, in the same way there's never been an expression of God's grace that wasn't unmerited.

Secondly, people often connect worldly views about worldly "favor" with the favor that sometimes accompanies God's grace. In today's society, favor is often used as a calculated gesture, not a free gift. Usually, when someone is shown special "favor," there's almost always a catch.

Whether the favor is shown because of a relationship, or perhaps because of the recipient's celebrity status, once favor is given, the old "you can't get something for nothing" rule is set into motion. In due course, the party extending the favor expects to gain something in return.

I'm not suggesting there's anything particularly wrong with using favor this way: in fact, this kind of practice is accepted in nearly every culture. However, I do want to point out (as strongly as possible) that godly favor is nothing like this—there's nothing *quid pro quo* about it.

Thirdly, favor is widely considered an action that mainly changes our *circumstances*. For example, a banker approving a loan for which you didn't really qualify. Or an employer who hires you over thousands of other applicants. In cases like this we tend to focus on how favor impacts the circumstances.

Grace *does* work prominently in our circumstances, but its greatest and most enduring impact is *internal*, not circumstantial. While it's true that grace works wondrously in nature and in our circumstances, the focus of God's grace has always been *people*. God's grace changes *us*. Like an elite Navy Seal team, grace slips past our defenses, penetrates the complex web of our innermost nature, and produces transformation in the most resistant and resilient parts of our soul.

Grace 101

Here's my definition of grace: *Grace is the discreet spiritual force that takes us beyond ourselves, working in us and around us to complete God's purposes and plans.* The following two passages are the joint anchors for my definition of grace:

> [Not in your own strength] for it is God Who is all the while effectually at work in you [energizing and creating in you the power and desire], both to will and to work for his good pleasure and satisfaction and delight. (Phil. 2:13 AMP)

> And we know that God causes everything to work together for the good of those who love God and are called according to his purpose for them. (Rom. 8:28 NLT)

The first passage (Phil. 2:13) makes it clear that grace isn't generated by anything of human nature. It's theological, not anthropological. It's not something humans contribute to. It's all God and it's all from God.

Moreover, this passage plainly shows that not only does grace provide the energy and resources to accomplish God's will in and through us, but grace even creates the appetite in us to desire God's will in the first place.

The second passage (Rom. 8:28) clearly shows that God orchestrates the circumstances of life (often anonymously) until they come into perfect alignment with his purposes. Circumstantial developments (that many people refer to as luck, good fortune, fate, etc.) are usually a matter of grace forcing the world to get in line with something that God has determined to do. This definition emphasizes three important aspects of grace.

First, grace is a distinct, often unnoticeable *spiritual force*. It's not a stroke of luck, fate, destiny, fortune, or some random evolutionary development. It's not a quantum hiccup in the course of universal events. Grace is a powerful force that gets the job done—often surreptitiously. I like to think of grace as God's velvet-covered sledgehammer.

Grace comes from God's heart—it's a willful and purposeful extension of his love. When grace leaves heaven, it comes to the earth with a specific mission to accomplish—it has an exact assignment. Grace is the unseen military force dispatched alongside God's words. This is partly what the author of the book of Acts wanted us to understand when he wrote: "Now I commit you to God and to the *word of his grace*, which can *build you up* and *give you an inheritance* [italics added]" (Acts 20:32 NLT).

Secondly, grace works simultaneously (albeit distinctively) in us *and* in our circumstances to bring about whatever change is needed. One of the greatest examples of this was the story of Moses.

Moses was one of the most unlikely choices to lead a nation out of slavery and into incredible blessing. When God called him to lead the people of Israel out of captivity, Moses was a wavering, insecure wreck. He desperately tried to get out of it, giving God every excuse he could think of.

Among the reasons he gave God were that he stuttered, he was intimidated by his wife, he considered himself to be slow-witted, he had completely embarrassed himself in front of these same people before, and he didn't think anyone would have any respect or confidence in him.

On top of all that, he had killed an Egyptian forty years earlier and was wanted for murder! Eventually he relented to God's call and, as the saying goes, the rest is history (see Exodus 3–4).

Everyone knows about the incredible miracles associated with this story. The ten amazing plagues, the parting of the Red Sea, the miraculous provisions of manna from heaven, and water from a rock that followed them around as they wandered through the desert.

These mind-boggling events literally bent nature over backwards, and were all brought about by the forces of God's grace. But even more durable was the makeover that grace accomplished in Moses' life. Grace transformed him from an insecure sheep-herder with a clouded past, into one of the most significant, courageous, and effective leaders in all history.

Thirdly, grace achieves *God's purposes* by means of *God's plans*. Not only does grace work to complete *what* God wants, but it also works to complete it *the way* that God wants it done.

Remember when God told a seventy-five year-old man named Abraham that he and his sixty-five year-old infertile wife would be the progenitors of a great nation . . . and that Abraham would be renowned as the "father of many nations?" God's *purpose* was to give them a child, from which a nation would come. God's *plan* was to heal Sarah's barrenness and to revitalize Abraham's ability to impregnate his wife—while building their faith in the process. God's purpose *and* plan were both clearly spelled out.

However, things just didn't appear to be working out the way that Abraham and Sarah had imagined. Ten years after receiving this promise, they seemed to be no closer to actually experiencing it than when they started. In an unpredictable turn of events, Sarah told her husband to start having sexual relations with their Egyptian servant girl, Hagar! Hagar became Abraham's surrogate wife and, in time, became pregnant and gave birth to a son.

Abraham and Sarah felt they could finally let out a sigh of relief—after all, their *household* had produced a son. They presumed this was the fulfillment of God's promise. There was just one problem. A small detail in God's original promise . . . something about the child being born of Abraham and *Sarah*—not Abraham and *Hagar.*

Thankfully, grace wasn't confused by this three-ring circus of rationalization, compromise, and weak faith. Grace eventually accomplished the miracle of producing a child from a hundred-year-old man and a ninety-year-old woman, fulfilling God's *exact* purpose in the *exact* way that God wanted all along.

Grace 201

Now that you have a broader understanding of what grace is, the next question is, "How do you get this grace to operate on your behalf?" It's a reasonable question—but an important one. The degree to which you enjoy your spiritual inheritance in this life pivots on finding the right answer.

There's really no mystery involved when it comes to how grace operates in our lives. Grace flows into our circumstances most commonly by reason of three different conditions. Let's look at all three briefly.

How Grace Comes #1: You Asked for It

One of the most common ways that grace begins to operate in our lives is from our *asking* in prayer. Enough grace for any situation is available to any believer who's willing to humble themselves (acknowledge that they need assistance) and come before God's throne with a simple request: "I need your help."

The book of Hebrews provides these clear, simple instructions: "Let us then approach the throne of grace with confidence, so that we may receive mercy and find grace to help us in our time of need" (Heb. 4:16).

This letter (originally written to a large community of believers who had previously been up to their necks in religious legalism) calls on us to take our eyes off our inadequacies and the challenges of our circumstances, and to redirect our gaze and our hearts towards heaven, asking the Heavenly Father to send grace into our lives and circumstances.

In following these guidelines, it's crucial to keep in mind that we're not just robotically repeating words like kids at a third-grade recital who have no real understanding of what they've memorized. Rather we offer these crucial prayers *in faith*, for only then do we position ourselves to receive.

Our prayers, offered in faith, will work wonders as long as they remain grounded in at least three truths:

1. Remember That God's Promises Are Unfailing.
Anything that God has promised or pronounced as his intent *will* ultimately come to pass. After studying Israel's history and all the original promises that God made to Moses when he led them out of captivity, Solomon made this declaration: "Praise the LORD who has given rest to his people Israel, just as he promised. *Not one word has failed* [italics added] of all the wonderful promises he gave through his servant Moses" (1 Kgs. 8:56 NLT).

Regarding his Word, God's track record is impeccable. He does what he says and he finishes what he starts. You have an assurance that his word will operate to your benefit and on your behalf—stand firmly on this fact!

2. Remember That Jesus Qualifies Us.
When it comes to asking God for grace, invariably the question arises, "Do I qualify for this promise? Am I worthy?" Let's settle these questions once and for all: no . . . and no.

In and of yourself you don't qualify and you aren't worthy to receive God's promises. None of us meet the requirements. However, we don't come to God asking for anything based on who or what we are—we come based on our relationship with Christ.

As believers, we're literally "in Christ," and by reason of our relationship and position in him, *we* qualify for all that he qualifies for. 2 Corinthians 1:20 says, "For no matter how many promises God has made, they are 'Yes' in Christ. And so through him the 'Amen' is spoken by us to the glory of God." Jesus' sacrifice on the cross satisfied any and every outstanding barrier that would keep God's promises from being available to us. Don't be moved from this fact!

3. Remember That Jesus Told Us to Ask.

When I was growing up it seemed that I stayed in trouble. I was always cutting up in school, trying to avoid doing my chores—it was always something with me. Because of this, I felt that my parents wouldn't likely say yes if I asked them to take us to Dairy Queen, the Zoo, or some other recreational pastime. So I'd ask one of my sisters (who rarely seemed to get in trouble—that's another story) if *they* wanted to go to Dairy Queen or someplace. Once one of them said yes, I'd go to my parents and say, "Avis wants to know if we can go to Dairy Queen." I figured if I asked on my behalf, I had little chance of getting a positive answer, but if I asked on behalf of one of the "little princesses" then we'd probably get to go.

The same kind of thinking comes into play when asking God for grace—we figure if we ask based on our own merit we'll probably get turned down. Jesus knew this would be the case, so he completely removed this roadblock when he gave us specific instructions to ask God for what we need—in his name!

Asking in Jesus' name isn't a religious formula or a liturgical mystery—it's a condition for receiving—and a commandment! Take a look at these verses in which Jesus addresses this very topic in great detail:

> I assure you, most solemnly I tell you, that My Father will grant you whatever you ask in My Name [as presenting all that I AM]. Up to this time you have not asked a [single] thing in My Name [as presenting all that I AM]; but now ask and keep on asking and you will receive, so that your joy (gladness, delight) may be full and complete. At that time you will ask (pray) in My Name; and I am not saying that I will ask the Father on your behalf [for it will be unnecessary]. For the Father Himself [tenderly] loves you because you have loved Me and have believed that I came out from the Father. (Jn. 16:23–24, 26–27 AMP)

From this passage, it's crystal clear that we can come before God in Jesus' name—based upon who Jesus is and how God views and relates to him. Our adequacies or inadequacies, qualifications or disqualifications, don't even factor into this kind of praying.

Because of this privilege in prayer, we can boldly and confidently ask for anything that God has made available for us, knowing that he'll hear and answer when we pray! Don't let anything persuade you away from this fact!

How Grace Comes #2: Just a Closer Walk with Thee

A second common way that grace begins operating in our lives comes from our lifestyle choice to walk in close, habitual fellowship with God. In this case, we're not seeking or asking for any special favor from God. We're not motivated by the presumption of any kind of reward. We're simply devoted to God for *who he is*—not what he's capable of doing.

Our devotion causes us to focus on how we can please him. His interests become our highest interests. We want to do what he likes . . . we enjoy his company. Being near him is both our consuming desire and our reward.

When we live like this, God tends to show his appreciation by dispensing grace in ways that are mind-blowing—unique to all recorded history. For example, the Bible records the case of a man named Enoch. Enoch was devoted to walking closely with God and pleasing him. God was so moved by Enoch's lifestyle that he simply lifted Enoch from the challenges and conditions of earth and placed him *directly* in heaven.

Enoch never died—he walked so closely with God that one day, while strolling on the usual pathway home, he took the first couple of steps on the familiar dusty path, but his next step landed unexpectedly on heaven's pavement—translated from earth to eternity in the blink of an eye!

There are many examples in the scriptures of astonishing and unique demonstrations of grace. For instance, Noah, whose lifestyle pleased God and caused God to select him to preserve the human race after the great flood. And who could forget King Solomon, whose only desire and prayer was to be able to honor God by serving as an effective leader for the nation of Israel. Solomon's attitude and motives so pleased God that God gave him the grace to become the wisest and wealthiest man to ever live—even though Solomon never asked for such!

If you're a parent, you can probably identify with this type of kindness. As a child I was on the receiving end of my parents' expression of this type of favor on several occasions. In one instance, my parents surprised me with a gift of an electric guitar.

I'd been working hard to get good grades in school, and I also did a lot of small chores around the house, including helping my grandmother (who lived with us at the time) and helping out with my younger siblings. I didn't even know my parents were aware that I wanted a guitar, but I received one without ever asking for it! It was a totally unexpected surprise, one that left me thankful and encouraged.

Even though this grace comes from God's kind response to our behavior, please don't mistake it as something we've earned—nothing could be further from the truth. God doesn't give us a system of specific reward-points that we can earn and later exchange for blessings once we've accumulated enough. Heaven doesn't have a customs counter or currency exchange desk.

Your attentive Heavenly Father, at his choosing, sends these unexpected gifts into your life as a means of showing you how pleased he is with your efforts and the way you're trying to live. It's a purely unique and uniquely pure demonstration of his goodness—it doesn't go beyond that.

How Grace Comes #3: Beyond Words or Deeds

The third—and most common—way that God's grace flows into our lives has very little to do with us. The Bible describes it like this: "This is what God does. He gives his best—the sun to warm and the rain to nourish—to everyone, regardless: the good and bad, the nice and nasty" (Matt. 5:45 MSG).

We all benefit daily from such demonstrations of God's grace. They can't even be counted. The things we so often take for granted, like the breath we breathe, activity of our bodies, a mind that can process information, cool breezes to refresh us, the ability to close our eyes and rest at night—the list is endless. These are all expressions of God's grace.

This kind of grace also includes God's divine protection over our lives. For instance, we'll fall asleep while driving on the freeway and "just happen" to wake up seconds before crashing into the car ahead of us. Or we go for a routine swim at the beach and suddenly get intense cramps in both legs; in spite of this we somehow manage to make it safely back to shore.

I grew up in one of the toughest inner-city communities in America and faced all kinds of dangers daily. Others all around me were caught by these dangers regularly. Some even lost their lives. But my life was always spared. It was by God's grace—and only God's grace—that I escaped the troubles that left so many others in ruin.

Unearned, undeserved, unfailing, unmatched. You can count on God's grace to be there for you when you need it!

Grace Yourself

Let's bring the two concepts—*spiritual growth* and *grace*—together. Different kinds of grace, as well as different measures of grace, are required at each stage of spiritual growth.

Think of how our body requires vitamin and mineral supplements because it doesn't naturally produce certain nutrients that it needs to function and grow properly. In the same way, our spiritual nature needs to have supplements of grace in order to function properly, remain healthy, and stimulate growth. Grace adds what's missing and what's needed. *Grace* makes *growth* possible.

It should be noted that while God's love doesn't have an expiration date, his grace *does.* Grace is similar to the manna that the Hebrews ate while wandering in the wilderness. If you recall, the manna had to be eaten the same day it was gathered—it couldn't be stored for the next day because it would always spoil during the night. Because of this, the people had to get up early each day to gather up a new supply of manna, which miraculously appeared each morning (see Exod. 16:15–35).

In the same way, God's grace expires over time. It has a specific, seasonal shelf life. The grace God gives you to deal with a specific situation may last anywhere from a few minutes to several years. This is why you can handle a difficult situation, in some cases for years, but suddenly one day the exact same situation completely knocks you off your feet—you can't deal with it one more minute.

The grace that allowed you to handle it previously has been all used up. You'll need to be replenished—to *Grace Yourself*—so you'll be able to continue to handle the situation or move in a different direction as God leads.

As we learn to walk in God's grace during each stage of the spiritual growth experience (including all the spiritual growth processes that run concurrently in our lives), we move steadily towards the image that God had in mind when he created us. He knows how long each of us will live on this earth, and he alone knows the degree of growth possible for each of us.

He knows the hardships we'll have to bear. He understands the pain involved in peeling away layers of dead, wounded, or diseased segments of our nature—a process that's necessary so newly generated, healthy segments can develop in their place.

God knows the joys we'll experience on the other side of a particular spiritual growth process, as well as the joys we'll bring to others. He also understands the pain of getting there. Most importantly, we have the assurance that more than enough grace is available at each stage of spiritual growth and at each transition point.

God lovingly and carefully watches over our lives and supplies the grace needed to transform us into the image he's designed for each of us. By the way, this *will* take a lifetime. Paul indicates as much when he wrote these words to encourage the group of believers in the province of Macedonia: "Being confident of this, that he who began a good work in you will carry it on to completion until the day of Christ Jesus" (Phil. 1:6 NLT).

It's never been God's plan for us to achieve perfection in this life—at least not as people normally define and measure perfection. Instead, it's his plan that we experience a life of continuous growth, walking side by side, hand in hand, with the one who cares about our growth the most.

So don't beat yourself up because of your shortcomings. It's understandable to be concerned that you're not yet able to consistently control your temper, stifle a negative tongue, get beyond a racist attitude, get rid of a nagging insecurity, or forgive someone who hurt you. Just remember that you're still in the middle of a lifetime of processes. This isn't an excuse or justification for your weaknesses—it's the truth.

God hasn't given up on you, so don't give up on yourself. Whatever stage or growth process you find yourself in, ask for grace often, and apply it liberally. *Grace Yourself!*

As I mentioned earlier, these growth processes take time—some take a lifetime. It can be discouraging to realize that you're still struggling with certain shortcomings. It can be frustrating, but don't be deceived by this. Don't let your faults define who you are, look instead to your strengths and to God's grace working in your life.

Don't fall into the "my-best-years-are-behind-me" trap. Who says your best years are behind you? Ask God to give you the grace and wisdom to take care of yourself as you age, but continue to remain vibrant on your journey. Don't settle for anything less—you'll be surprised at the things that still await you in the future. Take a look at just some of these accomplishments by some incredible "senior" citizens—all over the age of seventy-five:

- Jessica Tandy (age 80) won an Oscar for her work in *Driving Miss Daisy.*
- George Burns (age 80) won an Oscar for his work in *The Sunshine Boys.*
- American writer and physician Oliver Wendell Holmes (age 80) published "Over the Teacups," which displayed all his characteristic vitality and wit.
- Barbara McClintock (age 81) won the Nobel Prize in Physiology or Medicine for the discovery of genetic transposition.
- Christine Brown (age 80) of Laguna Hills, California flew to China and climbed the Great Wall.
- Michelangelo (age 88) created the architectural plans for the Church of Santa Maria degli Angeli.

No matter what age, you can always be growing, budding, branching out—right up until the moment that your life on earth reaches its ending. Samuel Ullman wrote: "You are as young as your faith, as old as your doubt; as young as your self-confidence, as old as your fear; as young as your hope, as old as your despair."[36]

The Bible gives us an even more assured promise: "Even in old age they (people of faith) will still produce fruit; they will remain vital and green" (Ps. 19:13 NLT).

The key is to Grace Yourself every step of the way.

Grace's Epilogue

The Grace Yourself anchor gives us a solid foundation in understanding God's methods for achieving whole-life transformation. He uses these growth processes to take us from a *"wretch undone"* beginning to a *"soaring on wings of eagles"* finish.

My prayer for you right now is that you find peace in trusting God's way, and that you learn and grow from what you've read in this chapter. Remember, this anchor encourages you to Grace *Yourself*— not your spouse, your child, a relative, friend, or associate. There's always the urge to rush out and tell someone else, "You really need to read this!"

Believe me when I say I appreciate the enthusiasm, but it's important to make sure that you're learning, growing, and implementing these principles in *your own* life. Don't lose sight of the fact that this book is written for your benefit *first.*

Annie Johnson Flint was a nineteenth-century American poet— one of the finest. Annie's natural parents died when she was a child, after which she and her younger sister were adopted by the Flint family. There she was introduced to faith in God.

While Annie was still in her teens, both her adopted parents died suddenly—within months of each other—leaving her and her sister destitute and orphaned. Annie was able to get a job as a schoolteacher, which had been a lifelong dream. But two years after she started teaching, she was stricken with severe arthritis.

The cruel disease twisted her hands until she could barely hold a piece of chalk. By her third year, she was unable to walk and, eventually, she became totally bed-ridden and had to be admitted to a sanitarium.

Still a young woman, Annie found herself crippled, broken, penniless, and nearly helpless. It was at this point that she re-taught herself how to hold a pen and to write, in spite of the gnarled, twisted condition of her hands. She began to write poetry—inspirational verses that were suddenly and unexpectedly birthed in her soul. At first, her writings found their way to a few Sunday school classes, a few local schools, and the local newspaper, but before long her poetry was being published and sold all over the country.

Annie's writings became increasingly popular, even as her physical condition grew worse. At the height (or lowest point) of her suffering, it struck her that while she was physically confined to a sickbed, God's grace had allowed her voice to travel unhindered all over the world. The magnitude of her reflections overwhelmed her.

Wanting to capture her thoughts, she asked that a typewriter be brought to her bedside. No longer able to hold a pen, she laboriously pecked out each letter, using her knuckles to press down the keys. The result was the following timeless tribute to God's grace.

He giveth more grace when the burdens grow greater,
He sendeth more strength when the labors increase;
To added affliction He addeth His mercy;
To multiplied trials, His multiplied peace.

When we have exhausted our store of endurance,
When our strength has failed ere the day is half done,
When we reach the end of our hoarded resources,
Our Father's full giving is only begun.

Fear not that thy need shall exceed His provision,
Our God ever yearns His resources to share;
Lean hard on the arm everlasting, availing;
The Father both thee and thy load will upbear.

His love has no limit; His grace has no measure.
His pow'r has no boundary known unto men;
For out of His infinite riches in Jesus,
He giveth, and giveth, and giveth again![37]

Grace Yourself.

Chapter 9

NOW
FAITH IS

Making Sense of the Seventh Sense

I was in a sporting goods store the other day when a weekend sportsman walked in and started picking out fishing tackle. He said he was excited about going deep-sea fishing for the first time. To the untrained eye, the gear in his shopping cart looked impressive. But, being an avid fisherman, I knew his fishing trip was going to be a huge disappointment.

The poles he selected were designed for freshwater fishing, not the kind of fishing he'd face on the ocean. If he were lucky enough to have a fish go after his bait, in all likelihood it would snap his freshwater pole in half.

But the chances of that happening were slim, because the lures he picked were for stream fishing. They looked nice, but would be useless on the choppy sea waters. Even though he chose expensive, top-of-the-line fishing gear, he was wasting money, which would later cause him to waste time.

Nothing in the world is quite as expensive as ignorance. Its hefty price tag consumes our dollars and our days. Dollars we can replace; days we cannot. The prophet Hosea observed that God's people are destroyed for lack of knowledge (Hos. 4:6). What was true then is true today: there's no shortage of poorly informed people among the ranks of the faithful, particularly when it comes to ignorance about the topic of faith.

Spiritual survival in the twenty-first century requires a firm grasp of *what* faith is and *how* faith works. Our murky views about faith contribute significantly to the Lost in Faith Experience.

Faith is like a two-sided coin. On one side, faith is the *actions* a person takes once they're spiritually inspired. On the other side, faith is an *attribute*—a sensory feature of our nature that *detects* something. In this chapter I'll discuss the sensory nature of human faith.

The Seventh Sense

We view the world through the prism of our senses. Five of these senses detect the physical realities of the universe. But the world isn't made up of just physical matter, it also consists of invisible and intangible realities that are sometimes overlooked, trivialized, misunderstood, or thrown into the bag of superstition.

Just as our eyes process visual information and our ears process audible information, our faith sense processes supernatural information. Our faith sense expands our perception of the world, bringing non-physical realities into focus. Faith presents this information to us in a usable format, giving us the chance to make better choices based on seen and unseen evidence.

God has given every person the attribute—or measure—of faith (see Rom. 12:3). Some of us have worked hard to develop this "faith sense," while others have allowed it to lie dormant and neglected. Unlike your bones or your feet, faith doesn't develop and grow automatically over time. Faith only grows by intentional effort. It must be trained in order to reliably assign accurate values to spiritual things.

As mentioned in earlier chapters, there are three parts to our nature; spirit, soul, and body. Each part has distinct characteristics and unique features, all which combine to help us enjoy life fully.

Our body is the "outer jar" which houses and preserves the spirit and the soul. The body also directly interacts with the physical environment. Our soul, among other things, is home to our intellect, memory, and emotions. Our spirit is where we find intuition and moral awareness. It's also the home to our sense of faith.

These three distinct facets of human nature make us who and what we are—unique and fascinating beings capable of experiencing life with an inward, earthward, and God-ward awareness.

To better understand the faith sense, let's compare it to one of our other familiar physical senses—hearing. Hearing is a sense that every healthy person comes equipped with; but the actual hearing experience differs from one person to the next.

Some people have hearing senses so well-tuned that they can detect sound on an almost superhuman level. Others have hearing organs that are damaged, defective, or diseased—even to the point of being completely deaf.

Some people can't hear high tones very well, while others have difficulty with lower frequencies. Some have trouble with volume or distinction of sound. Most of these hearing problems can be corrected. Audiologists tell us that 90 percent of hearing deficiencies can be improved through medicine or hearing aid technology.

If a person has a hearing problem and doesn't get it treated, they'll invariably miss what's being said to them and around them. They fail to notice important information that's spoken for their benefit.

In the same way, when our sense of faith is undeveloped or underdeveloped, we miss important information relevant to our lives. In some cases, the spiritual details we miss can make all the difference in what happens in our lives.

Let's examine a scriptural example of the faith sense at work:

> [6] "Now it happened, as I journeyed and came near
> Damascus at about noon, suddenly a great light from
> heaven shone around me.
> [7] And I fell to the ground and heard a voice saying to me,
> 'Saul, Saul, why are you persecuting Me?'
> [8] So I answered, 'Who are You, Lord?' And He said to me,
> 'I am Jesus of Nazareth, whom you are persecuting.'
> [9] "And those who were with me indeed saw the light and
> were afraid, but they did not hear the voice of Him who
> spoke to me.
> [10] So I said, 'What shall I do, Lord?' And the Lord said to me,
> Arise and go into Damascus, and there you will be told all
> things which are appointed for you to do.'" (Acts 22:6–10)

This is, without a doubt, one of the most spectacular conversion stories on record. Most of our spiritual conversions were simply a matter of hearing a gospel message, having a sense of personal spiritual conviction, followed by a trip up to the front of the church to pray. It was life changing for certain, but not necessarily spectacular.

Thankfully, the genuineness of spiritual conversion isn't based on how spectacular the experience is. That would produce a flood of dramatic, Oscar-worthy performances at the altar for sure—something that none of us want or need to see. Still, if any of us were actually knocked over by a great light and heard a voice from heaven ... that's something we'd never forget! It's also something that few people will ever experience.

Seeing the Unseen

Paul's testimony of this stunning encounter on the road to Damascus is a true example of the "faith sense" in operation. The things Paul saw and heard weren't natural. Even though he "saw" and "heard" them with his natural senses, they were detected by the spiritual perception that's only possible through our faith sense.

Notice the light Paul saw and the voice he heard had meaning for him *exclusively*. Verse nine of this passage shows that the people traveling with him didn't share his experience. They saw a flash of light that, to them, was a bright flare. The same light that left Paul blind for three days only briefly astonished his companions.

Additionally, Paul clearly heard the voice of Jesus Christ and, in fact, held a brief conversation with the Lord. In contrast to that, the men traveling with him only heard an unintelligible sound (see Acts 9:7).

Paul experienced something completely different from the people traveling with him. This spectacular encounter changed his life, but was only a frightening light and sound show to the others. Does this mean they lacked faith? Not at all. But it does give us a clue to an important lesson about our faith.

The experience was meant for Paul's benefit—*not* theirs. Your sense of faith is designed to help *you* perceive and understand spiritual things that relate directly (and in many cases, exclusively) to *your* life.

That's why two people can listen to the same sermon and come away with two totally different reactions. One person can be so inspired that he can hardly contain himself. The person sitting next to him can be so bored she forgets the message before the offering plate comes around. Our spiritual awareness, made possible through our sense of faith, detects what the Spirit of God intends for *us* at any given moment and in any given situation.

Our "faith sense" operates something like a television signal. The television station sends its signal out over the airwaves within a specific bandwidth. That signal is transmitted and received exclusively on that bandwidth range.

For example, in Southern California, the CBS telecast goes out on the bandwidth range that corresponds with channel 2 on our television sets. If I want to watch a program on the CBS network, then I simply set my TV dial to channel 2. As long as my television is tuned to channel 2, I won't receive signals from NBC, ESPN, or some other station.

Your faith has its own spiritual bandwidth and spiritual frequency. God allows certain spiritual events and information to travel on these frequencies specifically for your benefit. As you develop your sense of faith, it will pick up the legitimate spiritual information that's specific and relevant to your life—not just any random piece of spiritual debris floating around in the atmosphere.

A lot of people think faith gives a person open access to any spiritual activity around them. Many think that "spiritual people" see visions, angels, demons, have premonitions about future events, and hear voices—all on demand.

These are the kinds of inaccurate beliefs inspired by séances and gypsy-lore. The Bible is our reference regarding these matters, and based on the scriptures we know this is nothing more than confusing, spiritualistic nonsense.

There aren't any instances in scripture of anyone being aware of any spiritual activity that didn't pertain directly and specifically to their lives, calling, or circumstances. Moreover, most of the people in the scriptures who experienced any type of spectacular manifestation (particularly visions or audible voices) actually only had one or two of these experiences in their entire lifetimes.

Many biblical heroes (like David, Esther, and Samson, for example) had no record of any spectacular spiritual manifestations during their lifetimes. Spectacular spiritual manifestations are genuine, but they're rare—even in the lives of the most devout believers.

Needless to say, the development of your sense of faith won't transform you into a Cole Sear (the main character in the movie "Sixth Sense" who randomly saw dead people). The purpose and rewards of the faith sense goes well beyond the shock or entertainment value of spectacular spiritual happenings.

Rather, faith makes walking daily with God as effortless as turning on the faucet and as normal as pouring yourself a glass of cold water. Whether spectacular (as in the case of seeing an angel) or less dramatic (as in the case of opening your Bible to a passage that addresses a specific problem you're facing that moment), God wants to communicate with you through your faith.

Just as there are spiritual realities beneficial to your life, there are spiritual realities detrimental to your life. There are evil spiritual entities who seek to intrude and corrupt what you perceive through your sense of faith. They're like unwanted static or crosstalk on a telephone call. These intruders counterfeit the legitimate spiritual activities designed to aid us in life. They come for one purpose: to distract and throw you off track.

You can avoid being fooled, but it takes diligence. Evil spirits have very limited access to you. They're much more restricted than the legitimate spiritual things meant for your good. In the same way you can tell the difference between your mom's voice and the voice of a stranger, you can also develop your sense of faith to tell the difference between something that's spiritually legitimate versus something that's meant to deceive you (see Jn. 10:3–5, Phil. 1:9–11, Heb. 5:14).

The quality of your relationship with God plays a huge role in this area. If you ask God for a fish, he won't give you a serpent; and if you ask him to train your sense of faith, he'll safeguard you from being deceived (see Lk. 11:11–13).

As we saw in the case of Paul's conversion, as you develop your individual sense of faith you'll find there will be times when you'll have personal experiences that others won't understand or even recognize. Don't be alarmed or discouraged by this; it's actually par for the course.

It's also important to realize that no matter how cautious and prayerful you are you're still going to make some mistakes as you develop your sense of faith. At times, you'll miss it. Mistakes are simply part of any human learning and living process. Don't ever think that a mistake in this area is an indicator that your faith is flawed or disingenuous. It's simply a sign that your faith has some growing to do.

Remember, your spirituality is still a part of your human nature, and nothing of our human nature works perfectly every time. The virtuoso concert pianist will hit a wrong note from time to time. The basketball professional who earns $15 million a year will occasionally miss a foul shot. The Noble Prize-winning physicist will miscalculate an equation every now and then. Even natural processes, like breathing for example, will occasionally produce a hiccup.

When it comes to faith and spiritual matters, sometimes you and I are just going to miss it. Settle the issue once and for all—only God is perfect. You and I may be children of God and we may be created in his image, but we aren't perfect creatures.

Cultivating Faith on All Levels

Here's a list of fundamental guidelines to help develop your sense of faith:

1. Nourish your sense of faith—exercise it—constantly by studying, meditating prayerfully on the scriptures daily and *putting what you study into practice* (see Josh. 1:8, Psa. 1:1–2, Jas. 1:17).

2. Selectively share some of your spiritual experiences with (no more than) a handful of carefully chosen, proven spiritual mentors, friends, or spiritually mature people. Prayerfully consider their feedback.

3. Godly faith only operates through love (Greek-*agapao*—Gal. 5:6), and this kind of *agapao* love can only be directed towards a person (not towards a pet, a vocation, a house, a philosophy, etc.). Faith or love that's motivated by material things, goals, ministry, alms, ideologies or anything other than *a person* is more than likely misdirected energy that may get you in trouble.

For example, suppose you want to buy a van in order to take food and other supplies to inner-city poor people. Don't make the van the focus of your faith—instead keep your faith focused on the people who you want to help. Always associate your faith with the benefits it can bring into the lives of people.

4. Two reliable signs that your faith sense is developing as it should be are (1) you'll have a greater yearning to know God and (2) you'll have an increased concern for the goodwill of people around you. If you aren't growing in these two areas it's a warning sign that something's missing or wrong with what you're learning or doing.

5. Faith that operates by godly love won't lead you to be self-absorbed or narcissistic. Being the apple of God's eye doesn't equate to being the center of the universe.

6. Develop an intense sensitivity to the "inner witness" (the overwhelming sense of divine peace) that God uses to authenticate our faith experiences (see Jn. 14:27, Phil. 4:7, Col. 3:15).

7. Be accountable to other people (not only to God). Faith is powerful, and where there is power, there must be multiple levels

of accountability. Our character will seldom equal our intentions, and God's blessings will test the seams of our character like new wine tests the old wine skins. Being accountable to others will help make up some of the gap. For example, after the apostle Paul had his dazzling personal encounter (and several additional revelations from God), he respectfully and humbly sought out Peter and some of the other church leaders. He shared his experiences and his theological beliefs with them (see Gal. 1:18—2:10) and submitted to their counsel (see Prov. 11:14).

8a. As it relates to spiritual fellowship, don't be a lone wolf or a maverick. Prayerfully seek direction from God for a local church body to join—and submit to the leadership and authority God has established there.

The local church needs you, and you need the local church. Regardless of what spiritual advances you're able to accomplish on your own, your experience of faith will be enhanced by a commitment to a local group of like-minded believers (see Heb. 10:24–25). Remember the line from the classic poem "The Law of the Jungle":

> *For the strength of the Pack is the Wolf,*
> *And the strength of the Wolf is the Pack.*

Collectively, the faith community's strength lies in its diversity as well as its unity. Being part of a unified community that glorifies God *and* reflects the virtues of Christ is a great litmus test of your faith's maturity. Working with people will reveal the quality of your faith faster than anything I know of. Submission to godly authority and to one another is a precious and unmistakable sign of healthy faith.

Finally, I'm drawn to the definitive statement for understanding how faith really works: "But without faith it is impossible to please God" (Heb. 11:6). Our goals, thoughts and activities should be driven by a sincere desire to honor and please God. We shouldn't live our lives for the sake of approval by others, or for self-validation. Our greatest rewards lie in heaven. However, the things we do on earth to please God—to serve Jesus Christ—those things will last and provide a testimony to God's faithfulness to us for eternity.

And they can't be accomplished without your faith.

I really appreciate you taking the time to read this book. I hope it will provide encouragement, hope, and guidance for you for years to come. If you've enjoyed it, please consider purchasing one as a gift for a friend, especially someone you know in a leadership position (i.e. a parent, pastor, group leader, teacher, etc.).

I'd like to conclude with the following prayer:

Heavenly Father,
Today, may each step forward be taken with humility,
May each glance backward be seen through mercy,
May I bear my pains in truth and release them in faith,
May your light guide me away from darkness,
May trust in your word bring stillness to my soul,
May my eyes see the wonders hidden in each moment,
May my hands be strengthened for the tasks before me
May my words be seasoned with understanding and spoken
*   with grace.*
May your thoughts be my thoughts,
May your ways be my ways.
With your hand on my head, and your name in my heart,
Help me run well . . . and finish strong.

DIAGRAM OF
HUMAN NATURE

10 Functions of the Human Spirit

1. Inspires (gives life to, animates) the soul & body (James 2:26, Job 33:4)
2. Communicates directly with God. (1 Cor. 2:9–14)
3. The place of intuition. (Jn 16:13)
4. Seat of the Conscience. (Rom. 9:1)
5. Discerns and understands truth. (Job 32:8)
6. The legitimate throne of personal government. (Rom. 8:14)
7. Lodging place for God's presence. (Proverbs 20:27)
8. The birthplace of faith (2 Cor. 4:13)
9. Interacts with the world of supernatural/spiritual realities (1 Cor. 2:14)
10. Re-created at the time of the new birth. (Jn 3:5–8)

©Carl Prude 2010

10 Functions of the Human Soul

1. Collects Sensory Information [What I Perceive] (Deuteronomy 29:4)
2. Memory [What I Recall] (Lamentations 3:21)
3. Intellect [What I Think] (Proverbs 23:7a; Genesis 6:12)
4. Emotion [What I Feel] (1 Cor. 2:4–5)
5. Passion [The Intensity Of My Feelings] (Gal. 5:24)
6. Outward expressions [What I communicate] (Proverbs 29:11)
7. Place of Imagination [What I meditate on] (Lk 1:51)
8. Will [What I Choose] (Job 7:15)
9. Birthplace Of Creativity [What I conceive] (Genesis 11:6)
10. Controls the actions of the body [What I do] (Mk 7:15–23)

10 Functions of the Human Body

1. The "housing" for the spirit and the soul. (Genesis 2:7)
2. Is the temple of the Holy Spirit. (1 Cor. 6:19)
3. Gives us our natural outer appearance. (1 Samuel 16:7)
4. Is dying—literally perishing—slowly. (2 Cor. 4:16)
5. Goes back to the dust. (Genesis 3:19)
6. Is dead without the spirit. (James 2:26)
7. Lusts—has its natural desires and appetites. (1 Jn 2:16)
8. Is different from the flesh of animals, fish and birds. (1 Cor. 15:39)
9. Needs rest and sleep. (Psalms 4:8, Mk 6:31)
10. Needs natural, physical nourishment. (Matt. 15:32, Genesis 1:29)

ENDNOTES

[1] Diana Elliott, and Tavia Simmons, *Marital Events of Americans: 2009* (Washington DC: US Census Bureau, American Community Survey, 2009).

[2] *A New Generation of Adults Bends Moral and Sexual Rules to Their Liking.* Barna Group, accessed November 11, 2012, http://www.barna.org/barna-update/article/13-culture/144-a-new-generation-of-adults-bends-moral-and-sexual-rules-to-their-liking.

[3] James A. Swanson, *Dictionary of Biblical Languages with Semantic Domains: Greek (New Testament)* (electronic edition) (DBLG 26, #3). Oak Harbor, WA.: Logos Research Systems, Inc., 1997.

(Endnotes)

[4] Bruce Bickel, and Stan Jantz, *God Is in the Small Stuff* (Uhrichsville, Ohio[what state?]: Barbour Books, 1998).

[5] Bernard Ingmer, *Everything Must Change* (Los Angeles, CA: Almo Music Corp, ASCAP, 1974)

[6] Rudyard Kipling, . *If: Brother Square Toes,* (Public Domain 1910).

[7] Carl Prude, *Grandmama's Tribute* (East St. Louis, Il: Carl Prude, 2003).

[8] Encarta® World English Dictionary (North American Edition) Microsoft Corporation, 2009.

[9] Hannah Whitehall Smith, *The Christian's Secret of a Happy Life* (Ada, MI. Baker Book House, 1999).

[10] Henry Austin Dobson, *The Paradox of Time, Old-world Idylls and Other Verses* (Public Domain, 1893).

[11] Sir Walter Scott, *The Lady of the Lake* (Edinburgh: John Ballantyne and Co., 1810.

[12] James Strong, *Enhanced Strong's Lexicon* (G1401) (Oak Harbor, WA.: Logos Research Systems, Inc., 2009).

[13] G. Kittel, G. W. Bromiley & G. Friedrich, editors, *Theological Dictionary of the New Testament.* Vols. 5–9 edited by Gerhard Friedrich. Vol. 10 compiled by Ronald Pitkin. (2:261). (Grand Rapids, MI: Eerdmans 1964-c1976.((Oak Harbor: Logos Research Systems, 1997).

[14] Dr. Martin Luther King Jr., "Drum Major Instinct," a sermon preached on 4 February 1968 at Ebenezer Baptist Church. New York, Heirs to the Estate of Martin Luther King Jr, c/o Writers House as agent for the proprietor, New York, NY. Copyright 1968 Martin Luther King, Jr., copyright renewed 1991 Coretta Scott King.

[15] Alma Androzzo, *If I Can Help Somebody,* lyrics and music. London: Boosey & Hawkes, 1945.

[16] William Shakespeare, Macbeth, act 5, sc. 3, l. 42–7 (1623). OpenSourceShakespeare, Database © 2003–2012, George Mason University. All texts are public domain.

[17] S. I. McMillen, *None of These Diseases,* 3rd edition (Ada, MI.: Revell Publishers, , 2000).

[18] For a more thorough diagram of activities that take place in the spirit, soul, and body, see Appendix A: Diagram of the Nature of Man

[19] G. Kittel, G. W. Bromiley & G. Friedrich, editors, *Theological Dictionary of the New Testament* (Grand Rapids, MI: Eerdmans, 1964-), 963–967; and from J.

Swanson, *Dictionary of Biblical Languages with Semantic Domains: Greek (New Testament)* (Oak Harbor: Logos Research Systems, 1997).

[20] Melva Henderson, *Fresh Baked Manna* (Milwaukee, WI: Melva Henderson Ministries, 2010).

[21] Joshua O'Brian, *Mindfulness and Your Highest Human Potential,* altMed Smart Alternatives, January 31, 2010. http://www.altmd.com/Specialists/Meditation-Classes-and-Instruction-for-Everyone/Blog/Mindfulness-Meditation-and-Your-Highest-Human-Pote.

[22] Joel and Joanna Alvarado, *Breaking Free Ministry* (San Bernardino, CA: Rock Church & World Outreach Center, 2011).

[23] Please note that the word "compelling" in #5 comes from the Greek word *hagnos* and means "to be free from carnality."

[24] National Institute of Mental Health, Health Topics-Statistics (last accessed November, 2011) http://www.nimh.nih.gov/statistics/1ANYDIS_ADULT.shtml

[25] Federal Trade Commission, Consumer Sentinel Network Report January 1—December 31 2011. http://ftc.gov/sentinel/reports/sentinel-annual-reports/sentinel-cy2011.pdf

[26] Federal Trade Commission, Consumer Sentinel Network Report January 1—December 31 2011. http://ftc.gov/sentinel/reports/sentinel-annual-reports/sentinel-cy2011.pdf

[27] John Brown, *The Systematic Theology of John Brown of Haddington* ()Fearn, Scotland: Christian Focus Publications, 2002.

[28] Wikipedia contributors, "Temperament," *Wikipedia, The Free Encyclopedia,* http://en.wikipedia.org/w/index.php?title=Temperament&oldid=519998970 (accessed November 16, 2012).

[29] Wikipedia contributors, "Four temperaments," *Wikipedia, The Free Encyclopedia,* http://en.wikipedia.org/w/index.php?title=Four_temperaments&oldid=521760294 (accessed November 16, 2012).

[30] William Shakespeare, *Hamlet Act 1, scene 3, 78–82,* OpenSourceShakespeare, Database © 2003–2012 George Mason University. All texts are public domain.

[31] John Bevere, *Breaking Intimidation* (Lake Mary, FL, Charisma House, 2005).

[32] Romans 14:22b, 23b.

[33] William Shakespeare, *The Merchant of Venice, Act IV scene 1,* OpenSourceShakespeare, Database © 2003–2012 George Mason University. All texts are public domain.

[34] *It's You I Like*, © Fred M. Rogers, used with permission. (note, this is how the Fred Rogers Foundation specifically asked us to cite this, please see their instructions with the permission request form we received from them)

[35] Jennifer Riley, "Many Churchgoers, Pastors Struggle to Define Spiritual Maturit,". *The Christian Post Reporter,* May 11, 2009. http://www.christianpost.com/news/many-churchgoers-pastors-struggle-to-define-spiritual-maturity-38567/#ckaHouRbmqfJeg4P.99 (accessed November 3, 2012)

[36] Samuel Ullman, "Youth," in *The Silver Treasury: Prose and Verse for Every Mood* (Samuel French, 1934). Public domain.

[37] Annie Flint Johnson, *Annie Johnson Flint Poems, Volume One* (Grand Rapids, MI, Wm. B. Erdmans, 1944).